Losing Track

Losing Track

**Kerry Hamilton
and
Stephen Potter**

Routledge & Kegan Paul
London, Melbourne and Henley

in association with
Channel Four Television Company Limited

First published in 1985
by Routledge & Kegan Paul plc

14 Leicester Square, London WC2H 7PH, England

464 St Kilda Road, Melbourne,
Victoria 3004, Australia and

Broadway House, Newtown Road,
Henley on Thames, Oxon RG9 1EN, England

Set in Linotron Century
by Input Typesetting Ltd, London
and printed in Great Britain
by The Thetford Press Ltd, Thetford, Norfolk

British Library Cataloguing in Publication Data

Hamilton, Kerry
Losing track.
1. Transportation—Great Britain—Planning
—History
I. Title   II. Potter, Stephen,
380.5'0941   HE243

ISBN 0-7102-0575-9 (p)

Contents

To Dominic and Anna

Preface

Why do we travel? This may seem an obvious question but it is one that is rarely asked by those who provide our transport needs. To the individual the answer is obvious. They travel from A to get to B. They choose the way in which they travel from the wide variety of options open to them — walking if A and B are reasonably close; bicycle, car, bus, boat, train or aeroplane. But in reality does such a choice exist? If we think about a routine journey that we make to the shops or to friends, can we really choose how we get there or do the constraints on our travel determine where we go, where we live and what we do? If we were to devise an ideal form of transport what would it be? How would we really like to travel around? Are we content with what exists, with the effort and time that is expended on movement? Would any of our 'ideals' find favour with the government or the car industry? What if the distances between A and B could be reduced or eliminated? After all travel is rarely indulged in for its own sake. Why is it so often ignored that travel is extremely costly and should be minimised if at all possible?

Once questions as to basic travel needs begin to be asked and compared to that which exists the disparities seem ridiculous.

Transport is big business. It has grown massively over the past fifty years and the interests of the transport industry have a very strong bearing on what choices exist.

Losing Track traces the development of this industry and the way it affects people from the early days of railways through to current debates and political struggles over transport policies in Britain. It focuses on the powerful forces that mould travel in Britain today. The story has deep roots — we take it up in the era of the horse and coach when the transport industry hardly existed and few people had ever travelled on anything other than their own two feet.

Acknowledgments

We would like to thank Dr Philip S. Bagwell for his helpful and constructive comments on the draft manuscript. We would also like to thank the many people who have encouraged this project, in particular Winston Bond, Alan Grant, Dick Halle, Lawrie Harries, Neil Milligan, Sheila McKechnie, and Bill Ronksley.

The authors and publisher are grateful to the following organizations for permission to reproduce the photographs in the text:

Ford Motor Company (No. 44); London Regional Transport (Nos 35, 38, 45, 64); National Railway Museum (Nos 1, 2, 5, 8, 9, 11, 14, 15, 17, 19, 20, 22); The Post Office (No. 80); Stevenage Development Corporation (No. 57); Town and Country Planning Association (Nos 13, 39, 41, 42, 62, 81); Tony Wilson of Travel Lens Photographic (Nos 16, 18, 21, 36, 37, 43a, b and c); Tyne and Wear Passenger Transport Executive (No. 74); Warrington and Runcorn Development Corporation (Nos 55, 56).

1 Speed

The rash assault

> Posterity may be shot, like a bullet, by atmospheric pressure from Winchester to Newcastle; that is a fine result to have among our hopes; but the slow old-fashioned way of getting from one end of our country to the other is the better thing to have in memory. The tube journey can never lend much to picture and narrative. It is as barren as an exclamatory O! Whereas the happy outside passenger seated on the box from the dawn to the gloaming gathered enough stories of English life, enough of British labours in town and country, enough aspects of earth and sky to make episodes of a modern Odyssey.

So wrote George Eliot in *Felix Holt* (1866). The development of the railways in nineteenth-century Britain was looked upon with utter distaste by the coaching industry and the still young canal companies. This is not to be wondered at, for particularly regarding coach operations, the railways had massive advantages in speed and price. For example, the fifty-mile journey from Brighton to London took six hours by coach, but only two and a half hours by train. The coach at its cheapest was twelve shillings, whereas the train was only nine shillings and sixpence for travelling in greater comfort. The impact on coach routes by the opening of a railway line was often their total elimination. In 1835, the north Buckinghamshire coaching town of Stony Stratford, an important staging point on the London to Birmingham route, catered for 280 coaches per week. By 1844, six years after the opening of the London and Birmingham Railway, Stony Stratford's weekly coach traffic had dropped to 12 (Markham, 1975).

The railways did not only arouse the somewhat understandable opposition of coaching and canal interests, but faced a barrage of criticism from those with the seemingly modern stance of environmental protection and the social impact of new technology. Indeed all of the vital issues that surround transport developments today were remarkably familiar to the Victorian campaigners.

> Is there no nook of English ground secure from rash assault? Schemes of retirement sown in youth, and 'mid the busy world kept pure must perish; how can this blight endure? (William Wordsworth, On the Projected Kendal and Windermere Railway, *1844)*

Wordsworth's well known opposition to the coming of the railways in his beloved Lake District was more complex than it at first seems. In the early days of the railways he had positively welcomed them as a great human achievement which could enrich life. The later revulsion sprang from a disillusion with the results of the industrial revolution of which the railways were so vital a part. He was concerned not just with the look of the countryside, but with the question of the whole purpose of building railways. Who was building them and for whom? The answers he came up with disturbed him, for his earlier views on the social progress that railways could bring had been shattered.

The coming of the railways

It is impossible to say that the idea of a railway was ever invented at a particular time or in a particular place. The idea developed simply as an improved method to move goods, initially over short distances, eventually over hundreds of miles. By the beginning of the nineteenth century, fixed track was already extensively used in the mining and quarrying industries. The transporting of heavy materials in horse-drawn wagons over the same stretch of earth road soon made it impassable. The laying of wooden tracks to stop the formation of ruts developed into the first rail-ways. It was a simple, pragmatic approach which laid the foundations of a totally new method of transport.

Mining and quarrying also saw the first application of the steam engine, which from the early eighteenth century had been used to pump water from the workings. By the 1820s, with the development of metal rails and

1
Derby Canal tramline. Primitive railways survived well into the era of photography. This old tramline photograph gives a good idea of how railways developed from simple beginnings as a pragmatic method of hauling heavy wagons in places such as mines and quarries. (Photo: National Railway Museum)

2
A 1925 Stockton and Darlington Train. As part of the celebrations of the centenary of the opening of the Stockton and Darlington Railway, a full replica train was built. The line was primarily built for freight and many trains were actually hauled by horses. Passenger provision was limited and very basic.
(Photo: National Railway Museum)

lighter, more powerful steam engines, it became possible to combine the two concepts. The opening of the Stockton and Darlington Railway in 1825 is regarded as an historical landmark in the development of Britain's railways, as indeed it was.

The opening of the Liverpool and Manchester Railway in September 1830 was in every way a larger event than the Stockton and Darlington. It was the first modern railway, designed to link two industrial towns with an all steam operated freight and passenger service. This was no overgrown horse-drawn mineral line. The opening was attended by 50,000 people. Celebrities were there in their hordes, one of whom, the MP Huskisson, became the railway's first fatality when he misjudged the speed of an oncoming train as he crossed the tracks. And, for those who wanted a reminder of the opening, printers and pottery works went into overtime to produce endless

3
A Stockton and Darlington composite carriage of 1846. Twenty years after its opening, the quality of passenger provision on the Stockton and Darlington Railway had improved considerably. Most standard gauge railways by this time had adopted a three-compartment, four-wheeled design for their coaches. The central compartment is for first-class passengers, with two, somewhat more basic, compartments for second-class passengers either side. Luggage was carried on top, where also sat a guard. Third-class passengers were conveyed in open wagons. Some progressive companies even provided wooden seats in third class.

4a (right)
Britain's railways in 1845. There were ten main railway companies at this time, plus a number of small railway lines running a few miles of track. Note the relatively dense network of lines in Durham, where the first railways emerged in the 1820s.

4b (far right)
Britain's railways in 1870. By this time around two dozen major companies had established regional monopolies with fierce competition over long-distance routes. The network continued to expand through to the First World War.

reproductions of the event. The 'Rocket' and the Liverpool and Manchester Railway were soon imprinted on the memory of the nation.

The railways were seen first as an aid to industry, and passenger services took a low second place. But the response of the public to the new railways soon resulted in passenger revenue exceeding freight takings. This unexpected lucrative market was soon influencing not only the design of railway stock and stations, but the whole scale of many railway developments in Britain. The first big explosion in railway building occurred in the mid-1830s when over 100 miles of track were opened. By the mid-1840s most of Britain's major cities were linked by rail and by 1850 6,000 miles of track were opened. The pace did not slacken, for another 7,000 miles were opened over the next twenty years.

The enormity of the task of building such a network in early Victorian Britain cannot be underrated. Often the work tends to be portrayed as the product of mighty individual engineers such as George and Robert Stephenson and Isambard Kingdom Brunel. But these key men, whose contribution is there for all to see, were just a part of a complex organisation that had to be developed to cope with the sheer scale of railway construction. The engineering feats of the early railways were but one aspect. The railways were built by navvies with picks and shovels. The navvies were organised by contractors who managed these vast unwieldy projects. Navvies had to be paid, materials ordered and shifted, and work supervised. Everything had to be in the right place at the right time. Land had to be acquired and legislation steered through Parliament, with all the vagaries of the pre-reformed Commons (the 1832 Reform Act measures were very limited) and the deep-rooted vested interests of big aristocratic landowners. And, of course, entrepreneurs had to calculate and drum up the money to pay for the whole lot.

The organisation of vast industrial civil engineering projects had begun with the canals. To begin with, the railways took over this structure, including the canal construction labour force, the 'navvies' (navigators). However, this system of management and finance was crude and very much open to abuse. Effective project management and control only emerged slowly throughout the 1840s and 50s.

The enormous amount of money used to build the railways came from shareholders, and it is surprising to note how widespread share ownership was in Victorian Britain. Banks, manufacturers and municipal authorities helped to finance the railways, but the major new source of finance was the small shareholder. The railways had come at just the right stage in the industrial revolution. A new class had been created – the middle classes who managed and organised industrial Britain. They were seeking ways to invest their money and the railways presented that opportunity. 'Railway mania' took over, with even relatively poor people being caught up in the rush to invest in one 'lucrative' railway project or another. The middle-class woman 'of private means' in so many an Agatha Christie or Dorothy Sayers novel owed their living to the family shares, many of which were in a railway company. In one year £40 million was spent on railway building, a vast sum in an era when an individual could live on an income of £5 per annum.

The use of the money raised was subject to very little financial control, and it is hard even now to identify all the major frauds and swindles that went on during the 1840s and 50s. Many of the 'great' railway managers and champions were also unscrupulous charlatans who, although keen and extremely gifted in getting their railway built, salted away for themselves and their friends vast amounts of money.

Such practices were difficult to identify and correct, even as rail management grew in experience and financial awareness. Book-keeping methods were not designed to cope with such a complex enterprise as building a railway, involving activities in widely separated places all along a line. No point of reference existed for the price of land or the services of contractors. These varied immensely between different railways and it was difficult for the railway companies' managers to sort out what was a high price for a particular job and whether it involved genuinely high costs or the keeping of the chief engineer in a manner to which he was accustomed. There is some evidence that the lack of financial control significantly pushed up the cost of railway development in Britain. In the early years of railway building, the cost per line mile in was £31,000. In Belgium the costs were

5
A locomotive of the Taff Vale Railway. Would you salute this train? (Photo: National Railway Museum)

half of this figure and cannot be explained simply by differences in the kind of land to be crossed.

Management problems did not cease when the construction of the railway was complete. There were few industrial companies of the size of the railways and none had the same management problems of dealing with a workforce who were spread over miles of track, stations and yards, for whom supervision would be very difficult. The closest parallel was the armed forces, and before long the railways introduced a very military style of staff management. The Taff Vale Company's rule book of 1856 provides a good example of this. It required that its employees should keep their hair cut and warned them that 'not any instances of intoxication, singing, whistling or levity while on duty will be overlooked'. Employees were forbidden to engage in political activity and, by Rule 26, the employee was 'urgently requested on Sundays and holy days . . . that he will attend a place of worship as it will be the means of promotion when vacancies occur'. They were also required to salute their directors, officers and, in some companies, even the trains!

Although a vast amount of time and effort was given to tidying up and disciplining the workforce, the main reason for the unsatisfactory performance of many railway companies was inadequate management. Frequently the engineer who built the railway was brought in to manage it. Mostly they made poor managers and could not deal with the operational problems that beset the railway – freight getting lost, passengers stranded, co-ordinating complex train movements, replacing breakdowns, etc. Managerial innovations began to emerge once Mark Huish was appointed manager of the London and North Western Railway in 1846. He ushered in the era of the professional railway manager, but even so the 'good engineer/incompetent manager' syndrome continued for many years.

A gigantic waste

But no matter how sophisticated and advanced management techniques aimed to be, Britain could hardly be said to have a railway network as such. Although Parliament had to be involved in order to allow the purchase of land needed to build railways, neither government nor anybody else sought to co-ordinate the building of the railways. With the Board of Trade as its functionary, Parliament authorised all the lines that were built. The Parliamentary debates on each line were often lengthy, select committees on railways were numerous, and several Royal Commissions sat and debated. But the reason that the railways got this heated attention was less to do with Parliament's interest in the railways than the railways' interest in Parliament. The key role that Parliament played in getting railway projects off the drawing board and into reality meant that competing railway companies and other vested interests soon became adept at political gerrymandering. The 'railway interest' in Parliament was esti- mated at different times to number between 50 and 150 MPs, easily enough to topple a government in the days when party control was relatively weak. Some of these had been directors of railways before they moved into public life. Some existing MPs received invitations to the railway boardrooms, often to buy their support.

In *Railway Morals and Railway Policy*, Herbert Spencer, writing a century ago, described the role of vested interests in a remarkably modern- sounding way:

> Consider the constant pressure of local interests – of small towns, of
> rural districts, of landowners – all of them eager for branch
> accommodation ... Remember the influence of legislators, prompted
> by some of their constituents, some by personal aims. ... Observe the
> temptations under which lawyers are placed – the vast profits accruing
> to them from every railway contest, whether ending in success or
> failure. ... Conceive the urgency of the engineering profession, to the
> richer of whom more railway-making means more wealth; to the mass
> of whom railway-making means daily bread. Estimate the capitalist
> power of contractors, whose unemployed plant brings heavy loss;
> whose plant when employed brings great gain. ... Finally consider
> that the classes interested in carrying out new schemes are in
> constant communication; and have every facility for combined action.
> A great part of them live in London, and most of these have offices
> in Westminster ... clustering round the legislature.

Spencer was moved to write this primarily out of a concern to see railway shareholders' interests safeguarded. The concept of the 'public interest', with 'public' referring to the whole population, was given very secondary consideration.

There was little interest in co-ordinating or planning railway develop- ment, for Parliamentary concern about the railways just reflected the railways' own attitudes. The railway companies themselves were keen competitors, and although a company might be formed to build and operate a branch line off another company's main route, the order of the day was to co-operate as little as possible with the opposition. The result was a disjointed, inconsistent series of criss-crossed lines that could hardly be said to add up to a national network. What was more, there was no real desire to do so.

Even in very basic matters, like track gauge, the companies did not co-operate. Up until the Gauge Act of 1846, a variety of gauges proliferated: the Dundee and Arbroath was 5 feet 6 inches; the Garnkirk and Glasgow 4 feet 6 inches; the Eastern Counties and London and Blackwall choose 5 feet. No trains from one could therefore run over the tracks of another. But the greatest deviant was Brunel's Great Western Railway at 7 feet, swinging out from London to Gloucester, Bath, Bristol, Exeter to Penzance and St Ives. This and Stephenson's 4 feet 8½ inches on the Liverpool and Manchester and London and Birmingham were the main competitors as a standard gauge. Stephenson's gauge eventually won and all other track gauges were modified. However, progress was slow and the process was not completed until 1892, with non-standard gauge lines still being constructed well into the latter half of the nineteenth century.

The ethos of fierce competition and minimal co-operation led to a duplication of stations and routes, sometimes with rival companies building lines almost side by side. It was a massive overprovision which turned the railways from a potentially very prosperous industry into one where profit levels were relatively low. When, half a century later, the problems of this railway development process came to roost and Lloyd George's government had to deal with the mess, Lloyd George's verdict was that it had been 'A gigantic waste'.

The impact of the railways

The role that the railways played in the transformation of Britain into an urban industrial economy cannot be underrated. By the mid-nineteenth century, Britain was already the most urbanised nation in the world. The 1851 Census showed that for the first time the population of the towns and cities exceeded that of the countryside, something that had not occurred anywhere else in the history of the world.

Railway companies were among the largest enterprises in the nineteenth century and in terms of employment were very important. Towns like Crewe, Derby, Wolverton and Swindon were railway company towns and by 1901 the railways were employing over 82,000 people in their workshops building and repairing locomotives, carriages and wagons. Crewe was an entirely new town, built when the Grand Junction Railway decided to move their locomotive repair works from Edge Hill in Liverpool to a more central position. By 1901 the works employed 7,500 people and topped 10,000 by 1920. Wolverton, in north Buckinghamshire, was also an entirely new town, to serve the workshops of the London and Birmingham Railway when

6
Wolverton, north Buckinghamshire. The entire town was built by the London to Birmingham Railway and its successor the London and North Western Railway. Today the 'little red brick houses' give the town an atmosphere more in keeping with the industrial north than with the home counties in which it is situated. (Photo: Stephen Potter)

it opened in 1838. At that time a single locomotive could not make the run all the way to Birmingham and so engines were changed and serviced half way, at Wolverton. Within ten years it had a population of 1,500 and by 1901 had reached 9,200. Derby, an existing town, grew rapidly following the foundation of the Midland Railway's works, which by the 1890s employed 4,000 people.

But the growth of Crewe, Derby and Wolverton was small compared to the effect that the Great Western Railway had upon the little market town of Swindon. This grew from a population of 2,500 in 1841 to over 45,000 by 1901. Middlesborough, probably the most spectacular of the nineteenth-century new towns, was also a railway creation. In 1831 the area had a population of only 153. By 1841 it had risen to 5,463 and to 7,431 in 1851. The railways developed virtually every aspect of these towns, surrounding the railway works with tight terraces of artisans' houses. They even built pubs, schools and churches too. An idea of the character of such a railway town in the mid-nineteenth century comes from the writings of Sir Francis Bond Head, a colonial governor, who visited the London and North Western Railway (successor to the London and Birmingham) town of Wolverton in 1850:

> It is a little town composed of 242 little red-brick houses . . . a number
> of very large red-brick workshops, six red houses for offices, one red
> beer-shop, two red public houses, and, we are glad to add, a substantial
> red schoolroom and neat stone church, the whole lately built by order
> of a Railway Board, at a railway station, by a railway contractor, for
> railway men, railway women and railway children; in short, the round
> cast-iron plate over the door of every house, bearing the letters
> L.N.W.R., is the generic symbol of the town. The population is 1,405,

of whom 638 are below sixteen years of age; indeed, at Wolverton are to be observed an extraordinary number of young couples, young children, young widows, also a considerable number of men who have lost a finger, hand, arm or leg. All, however, whether whole or mutilated, look for support to the Company. (Quoted in Markham, 1975)

But the real impact of the railways was not in the towns of their creation, but the general effect they had upon the urban development process. Not surprisingly, the railways greatly affected the rate of expansion of established industrial centres like Leeds and Manchester, but by creating new markets, the railways sparked off the development of towns in the most unlikely of places. In 1801, the coastal Lancashire villages of Layton with Warbeck housed only 473 people which rose gradually to 943 by 1831. Sea bathing was becoming popular, so by 1841, the population of this area, now known as Blackpool, had risen to 1,378 plus 590 visitors. But it was the opening in 1846 of a branch line from the Preston and Wyre railway which really began Blackpool's rise to fame. Cheap weekly return tickets were available from Preston for half a crown, second class, or one shilling and sixpence third class. An 1848 excursion from Oldham cost as little as one shilling for ladies, but one shilling and sixpence for gentlemen. In the fifty years from 1857 to 1907 Blackpool's population rose from 2,500 to 47,000.

The influence of the railways upon the development of urban Britain varied from them being the direct cause of a town coming into being, through to more indirect influences of making the towns and cities that much better for industrial development. To a large extent, the railways only accelerated what was already happening.

They often had quite drastic effects upon the parts of a city they passed through. No railway company rehoused those evicted for railway development before 1880. This had a particular impact in London which, being Britain's largest city, required the railways to drive their tracks through already built-up areas in order to get their termini near to the centre. Somerstown is a particular example. Railway development began here in the 1830s with the construction of Euston, followed by Kings Cross in the mid-1840s and St Pancras in 1864. It was not just a matter of eviction, but the demand for low-paid labour at these big rail termini drew people to settle in what was left of the land between these stations.

The people most disrupted had least to gain. The average working man's income around 1850 was 21 shillings a year, which means that many must have been earning considerably less. Rail travel for such people was out of the question and, despite Gladstone's 'Penny Trains' Act of 1844, it was only towards the end of the century that the railways began to come within the reach of ordinary people. The railways may have stimulated the development of towns and cities and the availability of all sorts of employment, but they had little to do with increased freedom or mobility for the vast majority of these cities' population. The working class still got around on foot.

Although the mass of the population did not use the railways for regular travel, excursion trains were quickly developed by railway companies. Indeed it was this sort of rail travel that prompted the Duke of Wellington's famous comment that railways might 'act as a premium to the lower orders to go uselessly wandering about the country'.

But working men's trains were introduced late in the century, permitting working people (they were used a lot by working women as well as men) to take a very early morning train only and return on a specific evening train. The classes of rail traveller were not to be mixed! But the advent of cheap rail travel, together with the development of the newer trams and buses, was to spark off another phase in Britain's urban development . . . the burgeoning suburbs.

By the beginning of the twentieth century, rail travel looked like replacing all other forms of transport in popularity. It was within the reach of almost all to experience the magic of a first railway journey. For Fanny Kemble in 1830, it was the thrill of a lifetime:

> You can't imagine how strange it seemed to be journeying on thus, without any visible cause of progress other than the magical machine with its flying white breath and rhythmical, unvarying pace, between these rocky walls, which are already clothed with moss and ferms and grasses; and when I reflected that these great masses of stone had been cut asunder to allow our passage thus far below the surface of the earth, I felt no fairy tale was ever half so wonderful as what I saw. Bridges were thrown from side to side across the top of these cliffs and the people looking down upon us from them seemed like pygmies standing in the sky. . . . The engine . . . was set off at its utmost speed, 35 miles an hour, swifter than a bird flies. . . . You cannot conceive what that sensation of cutting the air was; the motion as smooth as possible

7
Somerstown. Little of the original Somerstown now survives, it having suffered bombing in the war and considerable subsequent redevelopment. This street is to the edge of Somerstown and gives some indication of the densely packed working-class houses that were built there.
(Photo: Stephen Potter)

too. I could either have read or written; and as it was I stood up, and with my bonnet off drank the air before me. The wind, which was strong, or perhaps the force of our own thrusting against it, absolutely weighed my eyelids down. When I closed my eyes this sensation of flying was quite delightful, and strange beyond description; yet strange as it was, I had a perfect sense of security and not the slightest fear.

2 Company and nation

By the turn of the century the railways had carved out a place for themselves in the life of the nation. Although the middle classes were still the main users of rail travel, the building and running of the railways paid the wages of 650,000 people, nearly an eighth of Britain's working population. Among these, some 82,000 were employed in the railway workshops, building and repairing locomotives, carriages and wagons. The conditions in the workshop, as in much of Britain's heavy industry at this time, were often terrifying. Industrial injuries were rife, including deafness, loss of limbs, burns, respiratory diseases and the all too common deaths.

Britain supplied, and often built, the rail networks of many countries, including India and Argentina. The reason why, uniquely in France, the trains on the Paris Metro drive on the left is because it was British engineers who built it! The workshops of Swindon, Crewe, Darlington and Derby supplied the world.

In 1910 the railways were still the dominant force in transport and continued to reflect the highly competitive conditions of Victorian Britain in which they had initially flourished. This concept of competition with very limited co-operation between railway companies produced problems for passengers and railways alike. Because many companies consisted of small regional 'Empires' the effects of competition were patchy, with a very good service being provided on some routes, and a poor service where the company had a local monopoly. If, as in many cases, a journey required a person to travel on different networks, the passenger might have a very difficult time in changing trains. Interchange had been made easier quite early on in the history of the railways when, in 1842, the railway companies established a clearing house system to facilitate through booking over different companies' lines (see Bagwell, 1968). Nevertheless, this really represented the very minimum level of co-operation necessary and in many other ways the companies positively sought to make interchange difficult in order to keep people on their own system. Poorly connecting timetables and the need to travel between stations to make a connection (instead of there being a joint station) are examples of this.

Consequences of competition

But problems for the railway companies as well as their passengers were not far off. Although the railways were now taken for granted they were

8
The Salisbury accident,
1906.
(Photo: National
Railway Museum)

operating in an atmosphere of financial insecurity. Many could not survive independently and were absorbed by the bigger companies. The numbers were contracting all the time. At the end of the nineteenth century 302 railway companies were listed. Two decades later only 120 companies remained.

Competition between the lines took on a new intensity as profits dropped. This competition had its sinister side, for accidents were often attributed to cost cutting leading to reduced safety. An accident at Salisbury in 1906 was attributed to excessive speed. The company involved, it seems, was trying to prove that it was faster than its competitors. At Ais Gill in 1911 fourteen people were killed in a collision between two trains. The cause of this accident was cost cutting: the use of ungraded coal led to a loss of power and halted the train at a crucial moment when it was crossing the path of another.

The clearest and most widespread examples of cost cutting causing railway accidents was in the failure to instal block signalling and continuous brakes. Block signalling involved a system of interlocking signals and points, which ensured that a train did not enter a 'block' of track until it was clear of other trains. It is an extremely safe system which, with modern modifications, is in use on British Rail today. Older, cheaper but less effective signalling methods were retained. Also the fitting of continuous brakes to trains was limited due to its cost. The effect of these two cost cutting measures upon accidents was staggering. A Railway Companies Association Sub Committee Report in 1871 noted that of 281 accidents on British railways in the years 1870 and 1871, 113 were caused by the absence of the block signalling system. This report had little effect. In 1889 the horrific accident in Armagh, in which 78 people were killed, would have been avoided had block signalling been installed.

The effects of inefficient brakes were less easy to pinpoint, as other factors could well have been involved in accidents. However it was generally agreed by the investigators of the accident at Skipton in 1874 on the Great Western Railway, where 34 passengers were killed, that this could have been avoided if the train had been fitted with continuous brakes.

These disasters were in some way a reflection of an industry with deep-rooted problems and a very shaky future. But the perilous course that the railways seemed set upon was suddenly changed in August 1914.

The railways at war

The popular presentation of war seems always to be in terms of armies and battles. Up until 1914, this approach may well have been valid, but twentieth-century war involves whole nations, not just their armies, as the entire economy and society shift their focus towards the war effort. The sheer logistics and burden that a country's transport system bears is difficult to imagine by a generation who have not, thankfully, experienced a country at total war.

All available transport was mobilised for the war effort. Even London buses were shipped across to France to transport troops to and from the Western Front. The government felt it necessary to take over the railway system and deploy it as one complete unit 'in the best interests of the state'. Control was placed in the Railway Executive Committee, a body formed in 1912 consisting of the managers of the ten leading railway companies, who worked under the general direction of the Board of Trade. The railways were by no means nationalised during the First World War. The government issued the Railway Executive Committee with military and strategic directives, but it had a free hand to carry these out.

The Railway Executive Committee had stemmed from a government report in 1911 which stated 'the era of competition between railway companies was passing away . . . the balance of advantage not only to the railway companies but also to the public would be found to attach to a proper extension of co-operation rather than the revival of competition.' This supported the view that railway organisation should reflect the realities of twentieth-century society, but this went very much against the ethos that railway management had grown up with, and until the First World War the railways' response to their deteriorating economic position had primarily been in terms of the old competitive nineteenth-century structures.

The scale and organisation required to fight a twentieth-century war

9
Women stacking coal during the First World War. This photograph was taken at Derby Loco Shed in 1917. The idea that women only replaced men on 'light' jobs during the war years is a myth. They undertook work requiring considerable physical effort and stamina, but which was generally of a low status. Women were also used to clean locomotives and stock. (Photo: National Railway Museum)

required the government to impose a twentieth-century organisation upon the railways. The somewhat ponderous nineteenth-century methods of management and the attitudes they embodied received a jolt as the railways addressed themselves to the nation's needs rather than the interests of shareholders. Despite moves to retain such a structure (Lloyd-George and Churchill supported rail nationalisation), the return to peacetime marked a return to the nineteenth-century railway.

The coming of the 'big four'

The experience of railway co-operation in the war supported the belief that a return to the pre-1914 attitude of cut-throat competition would be disastrous for the ailing railway network, struggling with low profits, worn-out stock and the strains of wartime operations. The railways were too important to the nation, as the experience of the war had shown, for them to be left to sink or swim like any small company. Equally the wartime operations had shown how appallingly inefficient the competition between the companies had been. In 1913 the 120 railway companies operated some 1,200,000 freight wagons. Under the Railway Executive Committee this stock of wagons was pooled and 80,000 were sent off to the Western Front. As the war progressed, thousands more fell into disrepair and yet the railways were carrying 50 per cent more freight, highlighting the sheer wastage and expense of the competitive structure of the railways. This not only undermined the viability of rail operations but, because as a consequence Britain had among the highest freight rates in Europe, it affected the economy as a whole.

The government was forced by these events to have more than an 'administrative' role in transport developments. In 1919 it established the Ministry of Transport, with quite wide powers to rationalise the railway system. But the railways themselves fought strongly against the initial idea of nationalisation. It took until 1921 to sort out what to do, with complex and heated discussions between the government and railway companies eventually resulting in the famous reorganisation of the 120 railways into just four large-scale groups: the London and North Eastern Railway (LNER); the London Midland and Scottish (LMS), the Southern Railway (SR) and the Great Western Railway (GWR). The mergers took effect in 1923.

But the 1921 Railway Act, although it did provide a better economic structure for the railways, had avoided the basic lessons of railways in the First World War. The Act did little to facilitate regular state planning for rail, careful co-ordination of rail development and a modern operational organisation. The response of the state was still largely within the nineteenth-century competitive ethos of railway operations. It was a patch-up job that only lasted for eighteen years before another World War once more brought about state control and paved the way to nationalisation.

Much has been said about the political and management attitudes to the 1923 amalgamations, but probably the best way to evaluate the true effect of this measure is to examine the effect that it had on the hundreds of thousands of rail workers and the way in which the new rail companies presented themselves to their customers.

The legal existence of the old companies may have terminated in 1923, but the legacy of a highly disciplined labour force and its tradition of company loyalty took many generations to break. A key part of the almost military-style level of discipline was the sense of identity that had been consciously fostered by management and reinforced by the adoption of company styles recognisable in the locomotives, rolling stock, architecture, uniforms and even office furnishings. Old loyalties, so much a part of railway life, remained and even today the pre-grouping companies have a recognisable presence, not just in the handful of preserved lines, but in the management structure and style of British Rail.

Old loyalties were demonstrated in events such as the 1924 locomotive trials held between Leeds and Carlisle. The crews of the London and North Western and those of the Midland engines competed against each other and partisan support ran to fever pitch. The fact that the two railways had by this time merged, and both crews were responsible to, and on the payroll of, the same company made no difference at all!

But if some employees ignored or regretted the 'big four' amalgamation, others were glad enough to lose their old management and hoped that this would lead to improved working conditions, better opportunities for promotion and the eventual demise of the old nineteenth-century authoritarian and paternalistic style.

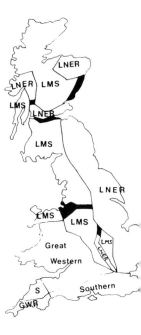

10
Areas covered by the 'big four'. The 1921 Railway Act largely provided regional monopolies for the Great Western, Southern, London North Eastern and London Midland Scottish Railways, although there were a few areas (marked in black) where more than one company operated. The greatest area of competition was between the LNER and LMS whose borders contained a number of major cities served by both companies. One of these was Edinburgh, and rivalry on the route from London was particularly strong.

Corporate image

The fact that the railways were run and managed after the 1923 amalgamations in much the same way as they were before it is reflected in the corporate image that the new companies sought to establish. Of the four new groups, the Great Western had least need to forge a new image as it was essentially the old Great Western with the addition of a few small companies such as the Cambrian and the Taff Vale railways. The public image projected was very much that of the old company with its associations of grandeur and exotic places. For the Great Western it was business as usual.

The London Midland and Scottish was far more of a new creation and the grouping was potentially prosperous, serving the main industrial areas of the north. Its management was very conscious of the company's reliance on these industries and the LMS became perhaps the most public relations minded of the 'big four'. In addition to the accepted practice of fostering company identity via locomotive livery, architecture, uniforms, etc., the LMS extended the concept in 1924 by employing Royal Academy artists to produce posters and even established its own film unit. It is interesting to note the way in which corporate identity was now being used not only to foster employee loyalty (a nineteenth-century management technique) but to foster client loyalty (certainly a twentieth-century marketing ploy!).

The London and North Eastern Railway inherited substantial problems from its component companies. Before 1914, the North Eastern Railway enjoyed considerable prosperity, monopolising transport between the Tyne, Pennines and Tweed with their basic heavy industries of mining, iron, steel and shipbuilding. The Great Eastern, spread through largely non-industrial East Anglia, had been less profitable.

At the time of the 1923 amalgamation, it was assumed that the old North Eastern would help to 'carry' its weaker neighbour, but in practice, if anything, the reverse was the case. With the onset of the depression, it was

11
A display of LMS Royal Academy posters. The LMS was particularly publicity-conscious, so it not only commissioned Royal Academy artists to design its advertising posters, but displayed them as works of art as is shown here.
(Photo: National Railway Museum)

12
Bracket at York station.
Even mundane objects
like this bracket to
support signals was used
by the railway company
(the North Eastern
Railway) to emphasise
its image.
(Photo: Stephen Potter)

the old heavy industries of the north-east that were worse affected. The south-east saw the development of the new light manufacturing industries with enormous suburbanisation around London spreading into Essex. The economic base for the railways was shifting rapidly.

The Southern Railway was London-based and much of its revenue came from commuter and holiday traffic. As such it was less affected by the depression than the LNER and LMS. Alone among the 'big four' the Southern carried out a very forward-looking programme of modernisation and electrification. Although economically better off than the other railway companies, this is not a sufficient explanation of the extent to which the Southern invested in new technology, particularly electrification.

Electrification is more competitive with respect to suburban lines than long-distance intercity traffic, but the impetus to modernise was very much due to the strong commercial management within the company. Elsewhere the power and influence of mechanical engineers ensured that outdated steam traction continued to be used, an organisational legacy that lasted well into the nationalised era of British Rail. It is true that the LNER 'Mallard', designed by the indomitable Sir Nigel Gresley, took the world steam speed record in 1938 at 126 m.p.h., but that was largely because hardly any other nation was bothering with steam for high-performance trains. They were all building diesels and electrics.

One example of the Southern's astute commercial management was the creation of 'Sunny South Sam' and the 'Sunny South Express' to promote tourism. The Southern had come a long way in using their corporate image as a marketing tool.

A square deal?

Although the government had balked at the idea of nationalising the railways, there was still extensive regulation of railway traffic. This was in marked contrast to the developing road transport industry, and by the 1930s, when rail's markets had already been badly hit by the economic depression, road transport began to inflict even further damage.

Under nineteenth-century legislation, the railways were obliged to carry any goods offered by customers. Charges were also highly regulated by the state. At the time these measures were implemented they made sense. They were designed to regulate competition between railway companies and to ensure that people were not disadvantaged by the railways' transport monopoly. But these regulations were not applied to road transport as it developed in the 1920s and 30s. Clearly the anti-monopoly element was no longer relevant. But the impact of these regulations on rail profitability was enormous. The 'common carrier obligation' required staff and special stock to deal with small loads of disparate freight which only generated a low revenue. Road freight, by being able to pick and choose only the profitable consignments, was at a considerable advantage over rail.

The smouldering grievance the railway companies felt at the legalised restriction on their freedom to choose and charge the traffic they carried came to a head when, in 1938, the 'Square Deal' campaign was launched. By this the four railway companies pressured the government to grant them the same degree of freedom in their pricing policies as was enjoyed by road transport. The Ministry of Transport was sympathetic to their case and new arrangements were being worked out with the railways when the outbreak of war intervened.

The 'Square Deal' saga illustrates the most contradictory attitude of successive interwar governments to the railways. The 1921 Railways Act

13
'Square Deal' poster on an LMS Railway Bridge, 1938. (Photo: Town and Country Planning Association)

that set up the four amalgamated companies was an extremely weak instrument and the state did not even reform its own railway regulatory powers as part of the 1921 Act. State investment in roadbuilding, including new stretches of dual carriageway 'arterial' roads, was at an unprecidented level, and yet by the Second World War even the most outdated Victorian rail regulation (which may have been causing more harm to rail than the 1921 Act ever addressed) was still stuck on the statute books. Throughout the interwar period rail income declined, and by 1939 two of the 'big four' were on the verge of bankruptcy (see Table 1).

Table 1 *Railway income 1928–39*

Year	£million	Year	£million
1928	45.2	1934	32.2
1929	49.3	1935	33.7
1930	42.0	1936	36.5
1931	37.5	1937	38.7
1932	27.2	1938	29.8
1933	29.5	1939	—

Sources: *Railway Returns, 1929–40* and *Government Control of Railways; Financial Returns 1940–6.* 1939 figures not available.

The Second World War

The 1921 Railways Act had only a temporary effect upon railway profitability, and by the late 1930s the railways were heading steadily towards the worse financial crisis in their history. The Second World War changed this perspective completely. As in the First World War, the government took control of all railways and this railway control agreement compensated the companies by guaranteeing them an income of £43.5 million. The railways were instantly rescued from probable bankruptcy. Within two years the sheer volume of war traffic pushed income beyond even this level, but the government then gained as they received any income in excess of the guaranteed level. As such, during the war, the government received nearly £200 million in railway revenue (see Table 2).

Although more thought had been given to the structure of government control of transport before the Second World War than had been the case in the previous war, the preparations made proved to be less than adequate. To a large extent this is not surprising as, with the fall of France, the war took on a very different complexion than was envisaged. The severe winters of 1940–1 and 1941–2 further added to the problems experienced by rail operations.

Before September 1939, the General Managers had expressed every confidence in the ability of the railways to carry all the extra traffic that

Table 2 *Railway income 1938–46*

Year	£million
1938	29.8
1939	—
1940	42.8
1941	65.1
1942	89.1
1943	105.6
1944	90.3
1945	62.5
1946	32.2

Sources: As for Table 1.

might be expected as military campaigns developed, but in practice there seemed to be no comprehension either by the railways or the Ministry of Transport of the planning that was necessary 'to fit together the complicated jig-saw puzzle of war-time demand for transport as a whole and to compare this with transport capacity' (Bonavia, 1971).

No new strategic lines, sidings or other railway works were constructed before the outbreak of war to cope with a different pattern of traffic. The only major work was on air-raid precautions, on which £4 million was spent in the last months of peace. Even this was as a result of the general fear of the Blitzkreig and was nothing particularly to do with the war planning of Britain's transport services. The planning of rail movements therefore developed as the needs of war impinged upon the railway's operations. Not only were the railways a key target for enemy bombing, but bottlenecks developed through the diversion of many imports from the vulnerable east coast ports to the more secure ports of the west.

The sheer odds against keeping the railways working effectively throughout the Second World War are difficult to comprehend some forty years later. All forms of transport were at a premium. Petrol was rationed and in consequence vast amounts of freight that normally would be transported by road, canal or coastal steamer were consigned to the railways. At the peak, in 1944–5, railway freight traffic had almost doubled, yet the rolling stock available had declined due to war damage, over-use or scrapping and the rate at which new stock was built never caught up due to the lack of resources for repairs and new construction. The stock of locomotives and wagons were strained almost to breaking point. In 1943 for example, the freight train load per train mile had risen from 121 tons in 1938 to 153. By the end of 1943 one of the four main line companies was operating nearly 500 locomotives which in peacetime would have been on the scrapheap!

It was not just in the volume of traffic that the railways were pushed during the war years but in the type and character of new demands that were put upon them. One of the first was the evacuation of nearly one and a half million people from areas considered to be particularly at risk from bombing, 600,000 from London alone. The majority of these were children, most of whom travelled by rail. It was a complicated exercise, involving a mix of local and long-distance journeys and the careful co-ordination of road and rail transport. But with no bombing occurring, and Britain entering into the 'phoney war' period of 1939–40, many of the evacuated children returned to the cities, only to have to be transported back again into the country when the air attacks did come.

The immense demands that troop movements made on the railway system was not always preceded by time for planning, such are the vagaries of war. The arrival of the first Canadian contingent in Liverpool in November 1939 was just a foretaste of the strain to come. By December of that year, a thousand men a day were crossing the Channel to Southampton for their week's leave.

The evacuation from the beaches of Dunkirk always invokes a picture of the amazing flotilla of 'little boats' that were organised and got across the Channel for that incredible escape of the British Army in France. Three hundred thousand soldiers were picked off the beaches and transported across to the Channel ports where the Railway Executive Committee had been busy assembling a pool of 186 trains to convey the rescued men to reception camps all over southern England. No advanced information was available of how many men were involved, or when or exactly where the trains would be required, yet the operation was successful.

The period following Dunkirk was characterised by the fear of invasion and the reality of the Blitz. Both impinged on the railways at all levels. As a precaution against a German invasion, station signs were removed or painted out in order to confuse any invading troops. With a large number of service personnel moving around areas of Britain unfamilar to them, the measure was certainly effective.

But at a more serious level, the difficulty of working under conditions of frequent air attacks put a great strain on the railways' work force. In the London marshalling yards, for instance, during October 1940 the alert was sounded nearly every night with the result that out of the 382 night-time hours, shunting had to be carried out in complete darkness for 299 hours. The trains were blacked out as well as the yards and stations. Tarpaulins were draped over the cabs of locomotives so as to exclude light. The lack of ventilation created a hideous working environment for the driver and his fireman of intense heat, condensation and air laden with coal dust.

Throughout the course of the Second World War there were 9,000 incidents of damage to the rail network. Railway track is relatively easy to repair. Should a bomb hit it, once the crater is filled in and new ballast laid, track laying is a straightforward procedure. During the war repairs of this sort were generally completed within twelve hours. But in urban areas, when buildings near the track and stations were hit, repairs took a lot longer and rail operations were severely disrupted.

It was not only the direct effects of the air raids that impinged upon the railways. Maintenance was severely handicapped because of the chronic

14
Bomb damage at
Middlesborough station
(Photo: National
Railway Museum)

shortage of materials. Poor grade coal had to be used and restrictions on steel and other essentials gave maintenance crews some of the toughest problems encountered on the home front. With railwaymen being called up into the services, there also developed a shortage of manpower. As far as the unions and men would permit, women took over many tasks, but they were not permitted to work on the footplate of locomotives. Despite this, working days of 18 to 20 hours became a feature of many rail workers' lives.

As the threat of invasion receded and with the entry of the United States into the war, Britain and her allies shifted from defence to the offensive. Air raids became fewer, but work loads increased and the tasks more complex. Troops and equipment had to be moved from camps throughout the country to ports to take part in the North African, Italian and, finally, the European campaigns. Supplies too had to be shipped out continuously, many of them beginning their journey by rail.

Preparations for D-Day involved complex and vast transport movements, and after the invasion even locomotives were shipped out to Europe. But then the air attacks began again with the V1 flying bombs and V2 guided missiles. Children were again evacuated from London and the railways suffered particularly badly through to the last V2 attacks in March 1945. There were 1,400 incidents and 102 direct hits on railway installations.

Despite the bomb damage during the five and a half years of war, the strains of increased and unpredictable traffic and the problems of low maintenance and labour resources, the railways had succeeded in operating

27

effectively. Against all the odds they had won through. War had shown that the railways were capable of great things. In one year of peak war-time effort, 1944, the railways were unrivalled in their carrying capacity, taking as much as 64 per cent of all traffic. When the entire transport system worked as a unit with a common aim, people and goods were moved as never before.

But it was war that had provided the unity in management and purpose. It was the war that had provided the exceptional support of the railways' workforce. This motivation could not be transferred to peacetime, but it was equally clear that the crumbling *laissez faire* operations of the pre-war railway companies had only received a reprieve by the exceptional demands and conditions of the war years. Stabilising the railways for peacetime operations would require a massive injection of capital. Not only was there at least £200 million of war damage unrepaired in 1945, but for six years all major improvement schemes had been shelved and the exceptional wear and tear to the network caused by wartime traffic needed to be put right. The railways at the end of the war were in a very sorry state.

Even before the war it had been clear that some adjustment in the relationship between the railways and the state was called for, but by 1945 it was becoming clear that quite drastic measures would be needed for the railways to survive.

3 Nationalisation

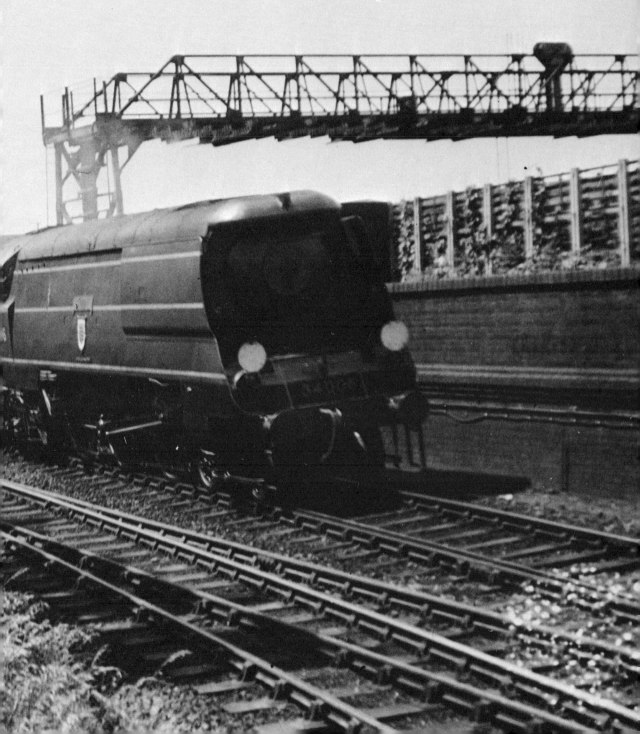

A new social mood

With the war in Europe over upon Germany's surrender in May 1945 Winston Churchill called a general election. Party politics replaced the national political unity that had existed throughout the war years, but the war had totally altered the political scene. There was intense excitement, particularly among the less well off, that the outcome of this election would decide whether the social reforms brought about and begun during the war would continue or disappear. The Conservative Party's manifesto, *Declaration of Policy to Electors*, offered some social benefits, but placed an emphasis on the need to guard against the totalitarian menace which it considered lurked behind the Labour Party's plans. The Labour Party's election programme, *Let Us Face the Future*, not only proposed major social reforms like the introduction of a comprehensive social security system and a national health service, but made nationalisation a key issue. Public ownership of coal, gas, electricity, the Bank of England and transport was proposed.

Transport was the giant in the list. It was not just nationalisation of the railways, but public ownership and control over the vast bulk of transport operations – rail, canals, road haulage, road passenger, ports and docks, coastal shipping and internal air services. Only by these being co-ordinated together, claimed the Labour Party manifesto, could they be operated 'at the highest level of operational efficiency'.

The general election was held on 5 July 1945. The results were not fully declared for three weeks, to allow for the forces abroad to cast their votes. The result was a massive victory for the Labour Party, surprising even their most avid supporters. Churchill may have been the leader needed for war, but he did not represent the national mood for reform and social advance that the war had produced. Labour's prime minister, Clement Attlee, upon his party's victory declared 'the Labour Party's great victory shows that the country is ready for a new policy . . . and we have the men to carry it out.'

With a large Labour majority, rail nationalisation was a very different issue in 1945 than it had been in 1919. The railways themselves were in a much weaker economic position and their political representation in Parliament had dwindled to an insignificant level. In 1900, fifty-three MPs were railway directors; in 1945 only two railway directors had a seat in the House of Commons.

But the new Labour government, despite its large Commons majority, had to work within considerable constraints. The war had strained not only the railways but the whole of the British economy. Wartime rationing continued into peacetime and with the cancellation of Lend Lease (the wartime loan aid agreement between Britain and the USA) in late 1945, Britain's financial problems mounted. Implementing a popular programme of social and economic reforms in the face of war debt, shortages and import restrictions was a daunting task. The period of austerity that followed the Second World War meant that Labour's plans were implemented under very unfavourable conditions. Most of the ministers in Attlee's government had seen service in the wartime cabinet and the strains of wartime leadership, added to post-war stresses, soon showed. By 1947 Herbert Morrison was ill. Attlee was in hospital early in 1951 and by 1952 both Ernest Bevin and Sir Stafford Cripps were dead.

Nationalisation's roots

Nationalising transport generated enormous controversy. Yet the concept and arguments for a nationally owned transport system had a long and respectable history. This was particularly so for the railways, where from the earliest days arguments had been put forward for state ownership and operation. As early as 1844 William Gladstone, then President of the Board of Trade and later to become one of Britain's most renowned prime ministers, was responsible for an Act which now bears his name. The Gladstone Act gave the government an option to acquire post-1844 railway companies after 1865. If taken up, this would have taken the vast majority of railways into state ownership, but this option was never exercised. Nevertheless, the principle of state ownership had been acceptable to Parliament.

The debate rumbled on, to be revived at the turn of the century with the formation of the Railway Nationalisation League in 1895 and the Railway Nationalisation Society in 1908. The emerging labour movement added to the ranks of these nationalisation groups. In 1894 the Amalgamated Society of Railway Servants (the forerunner of the NUR) passed a resolution at their AGM demanding railway nationalisation, and a decade or so later the Railway Clerks Association drew up a nationalisation scheme which was taken very seriously around the corridors of Whitehall. An influential book entered the arena when Alderman Emil Davis, a pioneer of the London County Council and a Fabian Socialist, published *The Nationalisation of the Railways* in 1908.

By the outbreak of the First World War, railway nationalisation was a respectable issue supported by members of the Labour, Liberal and Conservative Parties. The young Winston Churchill, as he was reminded *ad nauseam*, was a nationalisation supporter. He announced in 1918 to the Dundee Chamber of Commerce that the government were taking over the railways, clarifying the reason for state control in terms that are as relevant today for the concept of transport planning as they were in 1918: 'Railways in private hands must be used for immediate direct profit, but it might pay the state to run the railways at a loss to develop industries and agriculture.'

Churchill had latched on to a key aspect of transport operations: the concept of external costs and benefits (called 'externalities'). Transport operations result in benefits to their users and the areas they serve that do not necessarily benefit the transport operators themselves. For example, the construction of a railway line will raise land values in the area it serves, create jobs by making the area's industries more competitive and the labour supply more mobile, reduce unemployment levels and need for state aid, etc. These are benefits quite separate from the profits a line may make, though they may indirectly influence them. Hence only the state can make a judgment as to the overall worth of running a particular transport service. Internal profit or loss is only one component of this overall assessment, and a minor one at that. The ideological debate as to how transport should be assessed and planned has continued unresolved to the present day.

Churchill was premature in his announcement of rail nationalisation, but the fact that he made the mistake of announcing it at all shows how close the coalition government of Lloyd George was to nationalisation. At the eleventh hour nationalisation was abandoned in favour of amalgamation under the 1921 Railways Act.

The move to get state ownership of transport back on to the political agenda was championed by Herbert Morrison when he became Minister of Transport in 1929 in the first minority Labour government. The first area to attract Morrison's attention was London and his was the main force behind the 1931 London Passenger Transport Act which brought London Transport under public control in 1933.

The 1930s were a time when transport questions came to the fore, with the competition between road and rail becoming an increasingly discussed issue. Out of this Morrison produced two key documents, *Socialisation and Transport* (1933) and *British Transport at Britain's Service* (1938). These set out the principle that public ownership of itself would achieve little without the planned integration of transport services. In *Socialisation and Transport*, Morrison said:

> I am clear that the successful handling of the British transport problem is inconsistent with the continuance of the great number of conflicting ownerships and managements; transport must be brought together and its problems dealt with as a whole. That will enable us to destroy the biased railway mind and the biased road mind and to substitute a big transport mind. . . . Long distance road and passenger transport should be combined with the railways and the whole placed under one Public Corporation.

The main thrust of transport nationalisation by the 1945 Labour government was therefore to achieve integrated transport planning with the apppointment of a National Transport Board to co-ordinate state-owned rail, road, water and air services.

Resistance

The 'big four' railway companies resisted nationalisation, although the LNER, being financially the weakest, was very troubled by the possibility of a return to the pre-war situation. Realising that nationalisation was a real possibility, an anti-nationalisation campaign was launched at the height of the war, in 1942, by Sir James Milne of the Great Western. The Railway Companies' Association, realising that something was needed, began to consider alternative schemes which would retain private owner-ship, such as pooling of interests or a landlord/tenant relationship with the government. But beneath all these talks was the clear intention of the 'big four' to retain their separate existence after the war. When plans for nationalisation were announced in November 1945, these were met by total opposition from the railway companies.

The position of the Conservative Party was significantly different. They were prepared to accept nationalisation in some form, particularly of the railways, but they were determined to obstruct the road transport clauses in the 1946 Transport Bill. This indicates a view that, although the Conservatives considered that certain parts of the transport industry were in such a bad way that state ownership was inevitable, they did not share Labour's concept of transport planning and co-ordination. The road trans-port clauses in the Bill were subject to the most effectively organised and sustained critique of any piece of legislation during the Attlee government's life.

Leading figures in the Conservative Party, such as David Maxwell Fyffe, Harold Macmillan, Oliver Poole, Anthony Eden and Peter Thorneycroft, kept up an unremitting attack inside the House of Commons. Outside, they gave a large part of their time to attend functions organised by the Road Haulage Association and the Transport Users' Committee (a large body of employers and business organisations such as the Confederation of British Industry and the Association of Chambers of Commerce).

The Transport Bill was unceremoniously shoved through Parliament by the application of the guillotine to stop it being 'talked out' of time by the opposition. It was a large, complex Bill and the civil service was kept busy identifying and knocking the bugs out of it as it proceeded through Parliament. No less than 421 government amendments had to be inserted during its passage. On 6 August 1947 the Transport Act passed into law.

Organisation and management

It was the largest nationalisation project that Britain has ever seen. The 1947 Transport Act established the British Transport Commission to which all the railways (including their shipping, hotels, buses and other ancillary undertakings), canals, all privately owned wagons and some road haulage and road passenger concerns were transferred on 1 January 1948. The British Transport Commission were in effect owners and directors of the state-owned undertaking. Beneath the Commission were the Executives for Railways, London Transport, Docks and Inland Waterways, Hotels and Road Transport. (From June 1949 the Road Transport Executive was split into Road Haulage and Road Passenger Executives.)

The task of forming the various Executives varied greatly. The London Transport Executive carried on as before, having been in existence since 1933. The railways involved the relatively simple amalgamation of the 'big four' companies. Roads was the most complex area. Road haulage had to be created from scratch, involving many small firms. It was a mixture of the road services already operated by the railways and some companies acquired by agreement from the private sector. The latter included the passenger interests of Thomas Tilling and the Scottish Motor Traction Group. In all services involving a fleet of 14,500 buses and coaches were involved.

The members of the Executives were appointed directly by the Minister of Transport. The role of the Commission was very much one of strategic transport planning, with the individual Executives having complete control over their own operations within the Commission's guidelines.

This structure for nationalisation had arisen following a long debate over how nationalised industries should be organised and managed. The 1947 Transport Act was a far cry from workers' control. This issue had often been hotly debated within the labour movement, but was not seriously considered by Attlee's government. They preferred control by professional managers, not by workers or users. Workers' control was totally ruled out. The Cabinet was generally in agreement with Sir Stafford Cripps remark when he said, 'I think it would be almost impossible to have worker-controlled industry in Britain, even if it were on the whole desirable.' The Act provided for trade union representation on the Executive Boards, who would attend to 'industrial relations'. Morrison expressed the hope that 'trade union organisation and the process of collective bargaining will be more securely established.'

Overall, the trade unions seem to have been content with the provisions for nationalisation and their role in management. On the railways, improvement in the conditions of work soon resulted, particularly regarding safety standards. But many aspects did not change. The promotion pattern under nationalisation resembled quite closely the system that prevailed under the 'big four', where the public schools provided the entrants to management. After 1948 management training was given mainly to university graduates who came in with no railway experience. Promotion from the bottom got no further than assistant station master or, very exceptionally, station master of a small station. Even the trade union appointees to the British Transport Commission seemed to be isolated from their members. The pattern of nationalisation set in the 1940s in no way overcame the 'us' and 'them' aspects of workers and management, or indeed the 'us' and 'them' aspects of management and user. Labour and customer relations were little different to that of a large privately owned company. Users of

16
Under State Ownership.
An A4 Class ex-LNER
Pacific locomotive on
the East Coast main
line. (Photo: Travel
Lens Photographic)

transport did get a mention in the 1947 Act. One clause established the Transport Users Consultative Committee, which at least was a channel for views, even though it had no clearly defined powers.

If the 1947 Transport Act disappointed some of the most committed supporters of nationalisation, it was also criticised on more structural grounds. One of the errors which inhibited the integration of transport services was setting the British Transport Commission as the ultimate controller of transport while keeping the various Executives very separate from it. These tended to have an independence of outlook which positively hindered the transport integration objectives of the Commission. Yet the Commission had no direct control over the management of the Executives, who were appointed by the Minister for Transport. For example, the first Chairman of the Railway Executive was Sir Eustace Missenden, previously of the Southern Railway Company. He was a practical railway manager and there was no love lost between him and politicians or civil servants, such as Sir Cyril Hurcumb, the Chairman of the BTC!

Compensation and finance

Apart from organisational problems, the lack of capital inhibited improvements in the transport services of the Commission. This did not just relate to the generally poor state of the economy in the late 1940s, but to the compensation provisions under the 1947 Transport Act. For the railways, compensation was paid on the basis of Stock Exchange valuations in 1945–6. This was very favourable to the railway companies because the extra traffic carried during the war had boosted revenue and they had not got around to the much needed work of post-war renovation and repair. The 1947 Act treated this compensation like a loan, with a requirement for the Executive to pay interest as well as capital. So with compensation set at £908 million to be repaid over 90 years with interest of 3 per cent on the outstanding debt, the scope for repairs and improvements was very small. Despite the high valuation on their property, the railways had been incurring high trading losses. Just prior to nationalisation the railways combined trading loss had been £60 million, equivalent to over £1,200 million today or about three times the state subsidy that British Rail currently receives. If nationalisation had occurred a little later it seems likely that the railways could have been acquired for a much smaller sum than £908 million – from a Receiver.

The 1947 Transport Act was ambivalent about the question of whether the state's transport concerns should be expected to make a commercial profit or not. Despite the goal of transport integration, Churchill's 1918 stance that profit was almost irrelevant in evaluating the role of transport in a modern economy seems not to have been accepted. The British Transport Commission was required to break even 'taking one year with another' but the individual Executives did not have to. A loss from one could be theoretically balanced by a profit from another.

17
An ex-LMS class 8F 2-8-0 at Dawlish Warren in the 1950s. The railways suffered badly from low investment in the early years of nationalisation, with old steam locomotives and stock soldiering on. (Photo: National Railway Museum)

18
Class 77 electric locomotive at Sheffield Victoria Station on the Manchester–Sheffield–Wath line. The programme to electrify this line began before the war and was completed in the early days of nationalisation. The locomotives were the only electric design of the illustrious Sir Nigel Gresley, whose steam trains (particularly the A4 Pacific in Fig. 16) led the field in the 1930s. This particular locomotive, 'Juno', was built by British Rail in 1954. The electrification system used, 1,500v overhead cables, was soon replaced by the 25Kv system which made it difficult to integrate this non-standard system into the rail network. The line was eventually downgraded to freight-only status and when, in the early 1980s, the locomotives were due to be replaced, all but a short section of this line was closed. (Photo: Travel Lens Photographic)

The burden of high compensation payments, a wartime legacy of repairs and a virtual commercial operational brief meant that investment and progress towards transport integration was slow. In their 1949 report on the Railways, the British Transport Commission concluded that they could 'do little more than preserve their undertaking in a reasonable working condition.'

Some new investments did proceed, despite the lack of funds, but many of these were pre-war schemes suspended upon the outbreak of war in 1939. The Sheffield–Manchester electrification was completed in 1949 as was the 34-mile extension of the Central Line in London. Most of the tunnelling for the latter had been completed by 1939 and was used as bomb-proof factories until 1945. The Southern constructed much new stock in this period and even tried out the concept of the double-decker rail coach, before extending the length of many platforms to take ten- rather than eight-carriage trains.

Although the 1947 Transport Act had its weaknesses and fell short in its guidance to management, given time and good faith it could have become the basis of fully co-ordinated and integrated transport planning in Britain. Morrison believed that other political parties would support the state ownership of transport so long as it was efficient. The nationalisation of transport was not unique to Britain. Elsewhere in Europe nationalisation or the state control of transport was the subject of political consensus between left and right. Morrison's assumption appeared reasonable given that this seemed to be the way that modern economies were organising their transport services.

But in Britain, transport became a left/right issue and before long was suffering the fate of being a political football. By 1951 the British Transport Commission could not have been said to be far along the road towards the integration of Britain's transport services. Its greatest success had been in the building up of road haulage. By the end of 1951, the Commission had aquired 3,766 undertakings. The beaten-up lorries that had served during the war were systematically being replaced by new vehicles. But 1951 saw the Conservatives returned to power and almost immediately the denationalisation of road haulage was announced. The new fleets had to be disposed of, often to the same operators who had recently received compensation for their broken-down old wrecks. The cherished dream of Herbert Morrison of integrating road and rail transport was never to be.

4 Modernisation

The end of transport integration

When Winston Churchill led the Conservative Party to power in 1951, Britain's postwar economic recovery was just beginning to show. Indeed it was on a manifesto of 'wealth now' that the Conservatives had won the election. This was a time of great optimism and of a faith in a prosperous future for Britain's 'new Elizabethans'. Yet this vision of universal prosperity contrasted with the present reality of a nation still suffering from the effects of the Second World War and where economic growth was patchy and its benefits very selective.

The boom in consumer goods in the early 1950s occurred in a society where poverty and poor living conditions were still commonplace. New houses in the suburbs stood in contrast to the inner city bomb sites or the slums the bombs had missed, which nobody seemed to have the money or inclination to rebuild. The prefabs, intended as temporary emergency housing, had been patched up and were still in use. With petrol off the ration from 1950, car ownership and use surged to a new peak, catching the attention of the media and government alike. A new Ford Popular cost £390. This may give the impression that car ownership was cheap and within reach of the majority of the population but for many, £390 was getting on for a year's income. For the 90 per cent of the population without cars, public transport services were still suffering from wartime neglect and strain. Indeed it was in transport that one of the greatest contrasts in 1950s society was found.

Bus and rail services were still operated by inadequate numbers of old vehicles. Improvements had begun, but the sheer scale of the wartime legacy was difficult to tackle. The Korean War, coming so soon after the Second World War, made its demands on public finances, so too had other transport priorities like the replacement of clapped-out lorries by modern vehicles by the Road Haulage Executive.

To compound such a situation, the advantages it was hoped could be reaped from the integrated planning of transport were wiped out when the newly elected Conservative government, not surprisingly, sought to foster competition rather than planning in transport. Their aversion to state ownership led to the dismantling of any state co-ordinating and integrating functions, even of the transport services that were not returned to private ownership. With the 1953 Transport Act, transport planning at a national level effectively ceased and has never returned.

Under the 1953 Act, the British Transport Commission took on a totally different form. It became little more than an umbrella organisation to run the transport services that were in too bad a state to have private buyers. The Executives under it were abolished and it took direct control of railways, road passenger services, waterways and hotels, with road haulage being privatised. The London Transport Executive was retained, but as a separate entity, directly responsible to the Ministry of Transport.

The separation of the London Transport Executive from the British Transport Commission perpetuated the problem of the lack of integration between the capital's Tube and main-line railways. The two systems continued to be planned, managed and operated separately, with only limited contact to try to produce a system as a whole for Londoners. Serious attempts at integration only occurred when ownership of London Transport passed from government to the Greater London Council in 1969, and even today the two systems are very distinct and travel involving both can be difficult.

The canals could have become part of an integrated freight network, if they were assigned goods most suitable to water transport. Almost uniquely in Europe, Britain's canals have declined and, with one or two exceptions, exist purely for recreational use. Separated from a concept of integrated transport planning they had little chance.

Road transport was one area in which the British Transport Commission had made considerable progress over its short life. Since nationalisation,

19
LMS lorries delivering machinery to Victoria Mill, Accrington. Well before nationalisation, the railway companies had built up road services to act as feeders into their rail network. This applied to both freight and passengers. Indeed the railways were among the earliest airline operators too.
(Photo: National Railway Museum)

nearly 3,800 road haulage companies with around 40,000 vehicles had been meshed into an effective national company. This rapid progress was partly because road freight was in a bad way and needed priority but also because the process was a lot easier than the railways or canals who both had to maintain their routes (track and water) as well as run services on them.

Under the 1953 Act, road haulage was denationalised. The new fleet of lorries was sold off at a knock-down price, often to operators who only three years earlier had received compensation for their broken-down lorries. Parts of the Road Haulage Executive that did not have buyers were retained and a small nationalised company, British Road Haulage, was created out of these. This continued in the public sector until it was sold off under the Heath government in the early 1970s.

The 1953 Transport Act totally ignored the 'common carrier' problem of the railways while giving a boost to private road haulage. Even though it was meant to promote effective competition the Act was heavily weighted against the railways. Another area in which the 1953 Act adversely affected rail's ability to compete was in the use of road vehicles to deliver goods to and from stations. Up until this time, the Railways, and latterly the BTC, had provided for integrated road and rail transport with rail taking the middle leg of door-to-door services. The denationalisation of road transport broke this up and the railways were not permitted to run their own road services, supposedly in order to protect the privatised lorry operators from 'unfair' competition. In practice the reverse was true. The railways were even further away from their 'Square Deal' than they were in 1938.

Although still one state industry, British Railways' management was given a structure which harked back to the pre-nationalisation 'big four' companies. BR Regions, based upon the pre-1948 company networks, were given considerably autonomy and were answerable only to the British Transport Commission. But the real problems of the railways could not be solved by internal reorganisations. There was still an overriding need for new capital and a reform of the peculiar traffic carrying obligations that so inhibited rail's competitive position.

In 1953 the British Transport Commission was reporting that 'even the arrears of maintenance due to the extensive use made of the railways during the war have hardly yet been made good'. They were existing on a make-do-and-mend basis, crippled by a lack of capital and a lack of will at Westminster. Morale on the railways was very, very low.

The modernisation plan

It was in this context that Sir Brian Robertson, a very capable and astute man with a military background, was appointed as Chairman to the British Transport Commission. The rebuilding and modernisation of the railway systems of Europe had left Britain way behind. With his appointment the government wanted an idea of how Robertson might revamp the railways. Very rapidly he submitted to the government a fifteen-year Railway

20
An ex-LNWR 0-8-0 locomotive hauling a mixed batch of freight wagons towards the Tring Cutting, Hertfordshire, in 1950. By the early 1950s the poor state of the railways was causing concern in industry and very much influenced the Conservative government into supporting the Modernisation Plan. (Photo: National Railway Museum)

Modernisation Plan. This envisaged the creation of a thoroughly modern and efficient system, with the rationalisation and improvement of passenger and freight services and the total replacement of steam by diesel and electric traction. It required an investment of £1,200 million.

In a speech in February 1955, shortly after the publication of the Rail Modernisation Plan, the Chancellor of the Exchequer, Rab Butler, gave the plan strong support: 'It is in the interests of the country that more money should be put into transport. . . . Our policy is to proceed with the modernisation of the railways.'

This may seem a surprising reaction from a government that had shown itself so hostile to nationalised industries and no friend of the railways in the break-up and part privatisation of the BTC in 1953. But by the mid-1950s it was clear that the nationalised transport sector was of key importance to the prosperity of private industry. The concept of integrated transport planning may have been anathema to the Conservative government, but the effects of a run-down railway upon private industry could not be ignored. Many industries depended on an efficient railway service and wanted to see the railways modernised. The rail modernisation scheme was part of a general upsurge in government investment in transport in the mid-1950s that included the beginning of the motorway programme (the M1 was opened in 1959) and the encouragement of the development of internal air services. All of these were very much viewed as areas in which state investment would aid private sector prosperity.

45

In addition to the benefits to rail's customers, modernising the system could result in valuable contracts for private companies. This particularly applied to diesel and electric trains which were designed and built by private sector companies to replace the steam trains built in the Transport Commission's own workshops. This governmental insistence that contracts went to private firms adversely affected the modernisation programme as it got under way. Diesel locomotives were ordered from a large number of companies, many of which had less experience in building them than the BTC's own workshops. There was pressure to replace steam quickly and so fleets of diesels were ordered before there was a chance to evaluate their performance properly. In consequence millions of pounds were wasted on locomotives that had to be scrapped after a few years. The operational and maintenance problems of non-standard designs and non-standard components compounded the technological changes that the shift from steam to diesel involved.

It was not that no one in the private sector could build decent diesel trains. English Electric had been building diesels for export for many years and its Modernisation Plan locomotives had few problems. The company then went on to provide British Railways with the 'Deltic', at the time (1959) the most powerful diesel locomotive in the world. But government interference plagued the effectiveness of the railways to manage their investment funds.

Sir Brian Robertson gave particular emphasis to electrification in presenting the Modernisation Plan. Save for the Sheffield to Manchester route, no main lines had been electrified in Britain at this time. Sixty per cent of the Southern Railway's system of suburban lines had been electrified and a number of other electric suburban lines existed. The technology for mainline electrification had existed in a reliable and robust form since the late 1920s. Indeed, as early as 1918 Switzerland embarked upon a rail electrification plan, and by 1938, 90 per cent of their traffic was electrically hauled. The Belgians after the war had opted for an extensive programme of electrification, and by 1957 had completed a third of the system.

The system of electrification favoured in the modernisation plan was the use of 25,000 volt overhead lines, pioneered in France. At the time, this was a relatively new system and it was a bold decision to go for it. This turned out to be one of the best decisions made in the Modernisation Plan, for the high voltage 25Kw system proved to be much more efficient and economical than other electrification methods. It is now the standard system for European railways. The existing 630v system on the Southern Region of the railways was retained as this network was fairly isolated from the trunk routes proposed for electrification north of the Thames.

Electric traction has low running and maintenance costs, but is expensive, troublesome and time-consuming in its installation. Given this, and the desire to replace steam rapidly, it was clear that electrification was the long-term contender for main trunk routes and that diesel would be used as steam's initial replacement and for secondary lines. There was a brief dabbling with gas turbine power in the 1950s, with three locomotives

22
Modernisation diesel about to pass a steam-hauled train at Hatch End in 1962. RR C17 4-6-2 'Charles Dickens' and a C1 24 diesel. This line was later electrified under the Modernisation Plan. (Photo: National Railway Museum)

23 (right)
Soldiering on into the 1980s. . . . A Modernisation Plan diesel multiple unit train at Fenny Stratford station in 1984. A vast number of DMUs were built in order to replace steam quickly on suburban and rural routes such as this, the Bedford to Bletchley line. (Photo: Stephen Potter)

24 (far right)
The electrified West Coast Main Line (Photo: Stephen Potter)

21
*A Modernisation Plan
diesel train*. A 1962
photograph of a Class
42 diesel 'Pathfinder' at
Taunton hauling the
Torbay Express.
(Photo: Travel Lens
Photographic)

being adapted for passenger service (including one ex-steam train!), but this option was never seriously pursued until the advent of the Advanced Passenger Train in 1972. Even then gas turbines were dropped in favour of electric traction.

The main lines from London Euston to Birmingham, Manchester and Liverpool and from Leeds, Doncaster and York down to London Kings Cross were scheduled for electrification together with an extension to Ipswich of the already electrified London to Chelmsford line. A large number of suburban lines in the south-east, in the Glasgow area and round Manchester and Liverpool were also planned to be electrified.

As well as the proposals dealing with motive power, the Modernisation Plan outlined other development priorities for the creation of a modern railway system. These included track improvements (particularly the use of concrete sleepers and continuously welded rails), the extension of colour light signalling to replace the old semaphore system, and new signal boxes covering large areas of track, so requiring fewer staff. Passenger facilities were scheduled for renewal and improvement, including a number of new stations in areas, like the New Towns, that had seen rapid population growth.

Freight was the railways' biggest headache, and it was here that the Modernisation Plan resorted to its most radical proposals. It was envisaged that handling of freight should be concentrated in a relatively small number of very large freight yards. Many yards were on cramped sites with poor road access. New yards were to be built and a few existing ones enlarged while 150 others were to be closed. The methods of handling freight wagons were also planned to change. In existing yards, wagons were braked by hand, often requiring men to run alongside them to grab the brake. This was both inefficient and dangerous, but when the method was devised in the nineteenth century there was no alternative. In the new marshalling yards hydraulic jacks automatically retarded the wagons to the correct speed for them to be coupled to other wagons or to be unloaded. The technology worked perfectly, but came at an unfortunate time as methods of handling freight changed rapidly over the next decade rendering much of the modernisation investment redundant. Today standardised containers and specialist wagons have replaced the marshalling yards of the 1950s.

The replacement of pre-war stock and the groundwork for electrification were well under way when, in 1959, the government suffered an attack of second thoughts. What was behind this is a complex question, but the public stance was that they no longer considered the spending of £1,200 million on the railways to be justified. With many investments begun, but without the money to complete them, that investment was wasted. Bridges had been raised in order to cater for the overhead wires that were never installed. Platforms were lengthened for electric trains that never ran. Track works, signalling and junction improvements were left half completed such that any operational advantages were minimal. It was the typical mess that a stop-go policy produces.

With funds cut the emphasis shifted to one main area – the replacement of steam by diesel for both main and branch lines. The small-scale electrification to Ipswich was cut short at Colchester. The big Euston to Birmingham and Manchester programme did go ahead, though investment was slowed down and it was not completed until 1966–7. The electrification of the East Coast main line from London Kings Cross to Leeds, Doncaster and York was totally scrapped and so a scheme for diesel operations had to be substituted.

26
The demise of steam.
This diagram shows the percentage of track miles operated by steam, diesel and electric trains in Britain from 1955 to 1970. Steam's replacement was rapid, but with investment funds cut, electrification was slow. Primarily it was diesels that replaced the steam engine.

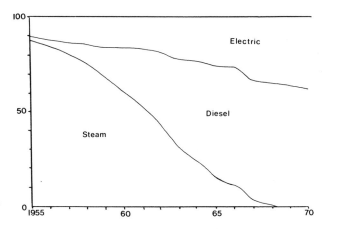

Elements of the 1955 Modernisation Plan did proceed. Steam was totally replaced by 1968, but track and signalling improvements proceeded slowly and many modernisation proposals were not even partially implemented. In real terms government rail investment in Britain dropped whilst elsewhere in Europe it grew. The motorways programme went ahead and was expanded; internal air services continued to be encouraged. Clearly the railways had been singled out for cuts. Why?

There were shortcoming in the Rail Modernisation Plan. One aspect that the government drew attention to when spending was halted and a review made was that the Plan's costs had risen from £1,200 million to £1,500 million. Although this may have been a reason not to increase the funds available, it by no means explains why they were cut. Inflation alone would have raised costs to £1,400 million by 1959, so the real rise was minimal. But in any event, the modernisation programme was halted until the production of the 1959 White Paper *Reappraisal of the Modernisation Plan* which advocated much lower spending on the railways. The same Conservative government was in power as had enthusiastically supported large-scale rail modernisation in 1955. The position of the railways had not dramatically altered, although there had been a drop in freight traffic. But the true causes of the 1959 halt to rail modernisation were not to be found within the railway industry itself.

During the 1950s car ownership and use had increased rapidly. Motoring was a growth industry, cars had become cheaper and more people than ever before were able to experience the pleasures and convenience of private transport. Car manufacturers, car workers' unions and car users were up and coming political forces.

To a government elected on a ticket of instant wealth, the car industry became increasingly important in the face of declining traditional industries. Coal mining alone lost 300,000 jobs in the 1950s and early 60s. The car industry was seen as offering the best opportunity for expanding employment and exports. It also very much fitted in with the ethos of 1950s Conservative thinking. Mass car ownership represented the 'you never had it so good' way of life and all that that entails, in contrast to the restricted life of the previous Labour administration.

Not only was the motor industry inherently attractive to government thinking in the late 1950s, but it had also organised itself into an effective lobbying force which was to be known as the 'road lobby'. Road interests had formed lobby groups right from the beginnings of the motor industry early in this century. The car companies and distributors had established the Society of Motor Manufacturers and Traders (SMMT), and road freight operators had formed the Road Haulage Association. They were all united in the overtly lobbyist British Road Federation (BRF). These groups had exercised influence over government before, but by the 1950s their power was reaching new heights.

The 1950s also marked a shift in power within the trade union movement. As traditional industries declined and light manufacturing (including the car industry) expanded, so the power balance in the unions shifted towards the Transport and General Workers Union (T&GWU). This was the union to which lorry drivers and car workers belonged, and before long it was supporting the pro-car, anti-public transport policies of the British Road Federation.

Paradoxically the political power of the road lobby was only strengthened by the problems and often frightening consequences of rising car and lorry use. Road safety, an issue long before the war, now became an obsession

27
The Hammersmith Flyover. Built by Marples Ridgeway, Ernest Marples's construction company. (Photo: Stephen Potter)

as the numbers killed and injured on the roads rose. Inner city road congestion and summer-time traffic jams to holiday resorts also attracted considerable attention. Road improvements were the simplest and most immediate reaction to these problems. It was an area of unquestioned state responsibility and one which was very much supported by the powerful motoring manufacturers and unions as well as the generally wealthy motorists themselves.

The rise in power of the 'road lobby' in the 1950s was rapid both inside and outside Parliament. It attracted support across the political spectrum, from the multinational car manufacturers such as Ford (who in the USA had been well used to such political approaches to stimulating the car market), to the car unions and the aspiring car owner in the suburbs.

The interests of the road lobby very much fitted in with the concerns of the government and before long the Ministry of Transport became all but the Ministry of Roads. In 1959 the rise of the road lobby was crowned by the appointment of Ernest Marples as Minister of Transport. Marples was the greatest self-publicist ever to hold this post and his background was entirely in the road building industry. He was a civil engineer and owned a road construction company, Marples Ridgeway, which included among its projects the building of the Hammersmith Flyover, the first major section of elevated road in London. Marples presided over the opening of the first motorway, and although its construction had begun some time before under a different minister (and was not built by his company), he sought to be associated with the motorways programme, coming to be widely credited (or blamed) for it. Given this road construction background, it is not surprising that Marples supported the expansion of the road programme and rail cutbacks.

Marples's speech in opening the £22.5 million, 75-mile stretch of the M1 epitomises the philosophical and economic strength of the road lobby upon (and within) the Conservative government of that time: 'This motorway starts a new era in road travel. It is in keeping with the bold exciting and scientific age in which we live.'

Being the Minister of Transport, Marples was not permitted to retain the ownership of his road construction company. Such a personal interest in the outcome of his policy decisions could not be allowed. He passed his shareholdings to his wife, which apparently he viewed as eliminating any personal interest or gain in his being responsible for Britain's roadbuilding programme!

The cutback in railway investment has to be viewed in this overall political context and had relatively little to do with what was happening within the railway itself. The road lobby, now well entrenched in Parliament, was effectively to take control of the railways.

Marples was a Minister of Roads. He was determined to see through a popularist road-building programme and did not wish to see anything stand in its way. In comparison to the costs of new motorways, the Rail Modernisation Plan was pretty small and really did not represent much of a threat to the viability of the car and road haulage industries. Nevertheless, Marples was determined to have a subordinate rail industry. When he became minister, he had received a government report which made no fundamental criticism of the structure of the railways. Despite this, in 1959, Marples set up an advisory group under the chairmanship of Sir Ivan Stedeford to examine the organisation of the British Transport Commission. Their report contrasted strongly with the earlier one on the way the railways were run and was highly critical, especially of the structure of management. It was thought that the railways could and should be run as a commercially profitable undertaking if only the top management would

28 (left)
The M1 in 1959. This photograph was taken shortly before Transport Minister Ernest Marples opened the M1 to traffic. (Photo: Town and Country Planning Association)

29 (right)
The M1 today. Note one carriageway closed for repairs! (Photo: Stephen Potter)

shake off its 'public service' mentality. This established the criteria by which the railways have been run through to the present day and totally sidestepped all questions of transport planning and relative state investments in different transport modes.

This report was what Marples wanted. The Transport Act of 1962 abolished the British Transport Commission. Management was decentralised with the Commission's assets being transferred to separate Boards for British Railways, Road Passenger, London Transport and British Transport Docks and Inland Waterways.

Marples did not have to look far for the first Chairman of the British Railways Board. He chose a friend of his who had been a member of the Stedeford Advisory Group and a severe critic of the existing management of the railways. At this time, Dr Richard Beeching was not well known to the public. His appointment to the BR Chair was an abrupt change of course, for he had pursued a highly successful career in ICI, becoming Technical Director. Save for his involvement with the Stedeford Advisory Group he had no real experience of the railways. The only aspect of his appointment to arouse press comment seemed to be concentrated more on his salary than his likely approach to running Britain's railways.

Few had even the slightest inkling that the appointment of Beeching represented the road lobby's conquest of the railways or of the disaster that was to overtake public transport.

5 Beeching

Railway closures were no new thing to the Britain of the early 1960s, for since nationalisation there had been a constant trickle of railway lines shut or curtailed. To a certain extent this was a legacy of the old competitive era and some lines were closed under the transport integration role of the British Transport Commission. But from 1953, with transport integration and planning at an end, lines came to be closed on narrower grounds, largely related to the level of traffic they carried. With the political tide swinging against the railways in the late 1950s, this minor pruning of the rail network was soon to change into a hatchet-job.

In the spring of 1960 the Prime Minister, Harold Macmillan, announced to the House of Commons the rationale to be applied to the railways:

> The railway system must be remodelled to meet current needs and the modernisation plan must be adapted to this new shape. This will involve certain sacrifices of convenience, for example, in the reduction of uneconomic services.

The 1962 Transport Act put this rationale into practice. It was intended to focus management attention on to the operation of the railways as a commercial enterprise. The newly established British Railways Board became directly responsible to the Minister of Transport and, at last, the railways were given a measure of freedom to pick and choose the traffic they wished to carry and to fix fares and charges. The historic common carrier obligations were abolished.

As the British Railways Board's first chairman, Dr Richard Beeching had the task of advising the government on how to change the railways so as to enable them to pay their way. His report, *The Reshaping of British Railways*, was published in 1963 and soon became known as the 'Beeching Report'. The Beeching Report was not just a shopping list of railway closures, but did provide an analysis of the role of the railways in Britain. However, the criteria and methods adopted to evaluate the role of the railways meant that major closures were a foregone conclusion.

For example, the relationship between road and rail was considered only to the extent that Beeching felt free to suggest that unprofitable rail services could be transferred to road. The possible effects on roads and whether it would require more to be spent on roads to accommodate such traffic than would be spent on the railways was not examined. He concentrated attention on the cost of retaining railways and gave no consideration to the costs and consequences associated with developing the road network.

One of Beeching's most vigorous critics, the late Lord Stonham, made just this point in the House of Lords. After giving his own estimate of the costs of road construction and maintenance, traffic policing, accidents and congestion, he concluded that 'if you reduce the receipts from fuel duties and vehicle taxes it reveals a net subsidy to road transport of over £600 million a year, four times the railway deficit.'

Lord Stonham's criticism struck at the heart of the government's attitude towards the railways. The lack of any clear economic or social criteria for the lavish state funding of road transport stood in marked contrast to the narrow commercial criteria for the railways. The argument that behind Beeching and the 1962 Transport Act lay nothing but political bias and the power of the road lobby has never been refuted and no satisfactory alternative explanation has ever been offered.

The Beeching Report made no satisfactory explanation of social aspects of transport, for example the problems of the urban commuter. As Colin Buchanan's report *Traffic in Towns* (published a few months after the Beeching Report) showed, if all commuting traffic were to shift over to the car then cities of over 300,000 people would require both massive urban motorways and the total rebuilding of the whole of their central areas. Commuting cannot be viewed narrowly in terms of the effects upon the railway alone.

The Beeching Report's specific proposals centred on four key aspects of railway cost:

1 The closure of over 2,000 stations, lines and services, involving the closure of one third of the rail network.
2 The raising of fares on commuter lines so as 'to reduce overcrowding'.

30
Winslow station, Buckinghamshire. The rail link from Oxford to Cambridge closed under the Beeching Plan in the late 1960s. The eastern end, from Bedford to Cambridge was totally closed, with the tracks being lifted and the land sold. The withdrawal of passenger services over the central section, from Bletchley to Bedford, was successfully resisted and remained open (see Fig. 23 on p. 47). Winslow is on the western (Bletchley–Oxford) section of the line, which continued to carry freight after the passenger service was withdrawn on 1 January 1968. Today there is one bus a day between Winslow and Bletchley. (Photo: Stephen Potter)

3 Reduction in rolling stock and the continued substitution of diesel for steam traction.
4 Modernising and remodelling of freight services.

The Beeching Report was very optimistic as to rail's ability to retain freight and passenger traffic on a vastly reduced network. Basically it viewed the railways withdrawing from long- and short-haul distance passenger services to be replaced by the car, bus and aircraft. An exception was urban commuter services, which nevertheless were to experience large rises in fares. The only future for passenger services was seen on medium-distance intercity routes. For freight, rail was envisaged to concentrate on bulk movements.

The effect of the Beeching closures and the attitude towards the railways that it represented clearly reduced the role of rail in Britain's economy and society. The road lobby's power to suck away government funding from non-road schemes had reached its fulfilment. But it was at the local level that the effect and hardship of rail closures can be most readily appreciated.

The customer 'watchdogs' established under the 1947 Transport Act were the Transport Users Consultative Committees. The grounds on which they could oppose railway closures were considerably curtailed under Marples's 1962 Transport Act to the hardship arising out of the shutting of a particular line or station. Considerations such as alternative costs, trade, employment or congestion did not come within their purview. Hence the common ground and links between the national efforts to oppose Beeching's proposals and local campaigns for an individual line were limited.

An example of a successful campaign to oppose the closure of a passenger service was the case of the North London Line, running from Richmond,

31
Camden Road station, on the North London line

32a (right)
*British Rail passenger
network, 1963*

32b (far right)
*British Rail passenger
network, 1984*

around London's inner suburbs (Kew, Acton, Hampstead and Highbury) to Broad Street in the City of London. The factors that led to this campaign being successful were not so much related to the issues of closure as to the organisation of the Hampstead Action Committee which ran the campaign.

The Committee was set up in response to some users of the line discovering that it was earmarked for closure in Beeching's *Reshaping of British Railways* report. There was thus an established organisation dedicated to the retention of the passenger service well before the closure notice was issued. In many cases, the local community and rail users were unaware of the threat of closure until the closure notice was issued, and by then it was difficult to pull together the resources and information for an effective campaign of opposition.

Even the Hampstead Action Committee had its difficulties in obtaining information from British Railways in order to make their case. Basic information, such as passenger usage, revenue and costs, were difficult to obtain, despite the fact that this information must have been readily to hand. The Committee organised their own research and effectively conducted one of the first cost-benefit studies to be done on a specific line, involving detailed surveys of schools, factories along the route, and of the line's users.

But the Committee's real strength lay in its political organisation. The line ran through a number of marginal parliamentary seats, held by all parties. The Committee itself included among its members journalists, people working for British Railways and others with good political and professional connections. They were successful; the closure was initially delayed and then, in June 1965, the repreive for the North London Line was announced.

There was no real transport planning reason why the North London Line should have survived whereas so many others closed. The reason lay primarily in the organisation, research, publicity and political effectiveness of its Action Committee. Ironically, today part of the North London Line is again under notice of closure. British Rail plan to extend the line over newly electrified tracks to North Woolwich and so improve rail links to the developing docklands. This will involve the diversion of services away from the line's terminus at Broad Street in the City of London, which is strongly resented by the North London Line's existing users.

The Settle to Carlisle line was also due for closure under Beeching's axe, with British Railways formally announcing the withdrawal of services in 1964. That the line survived to become the subject of another closure battle some twenty years later was largely due to the intervention of the West Riding County Council. But what was more disturbing about the Settle–Carlisle saga was the sheer lack of commitment shown by British Rail to this line once the decision to retain it had been made. The services suffered from lack of advertising despite the large tourist potential of this very scenic route. The Ramblers Association and other bodies have organised excursion trains on the line, but British Rail itself did nothing to promote traffic. Indeed, the withdrawal of regional services using the route and a lack of maintenance paved the way for the 1984 proposals to shut the line once more.

In other cases where rail closures have been successfully opposed, the attitude of British Rail has been more positive. In 1964 an inquiry into the proposed closure of the Fort William to Mallaig line resulted in its retention and the 1973 campaign around the threat to close the line from Inverness to Kyle of Lochalsh was also successful. This campaign emphasised the very special needs of the remote areas that this line served and the poor road communications, often cut by snow in winter. The 1962 Transport Act had restricted grounds for objection to that of 'hardship' and in the case of both the Kyle and Mallaig lines, the groups fighting the closure clearly presented very good cases. British Rail has since successfully promoted both of these lines for tourism and in 1984–5 a pioneering scheme of radio signalling was installed on the Kyle line as part of a programme of investment on this route. The future of both lines now seems reasonably secure.

The lifting of the threat of closure for the services that were saved in the Beeching round of cuts by no means ended the role of the groups formed to support their local line. Very often they became the public's voice in promoting the line and liaising with British Rail for improvements so as

to exploit the potential of the route. Very often such groups have taken on tasks such as transport integration and planning that have been neglected by local authorities. Often it has only been as a result of the work of such groups that bus and train services have come to be co-ordinated in some areas.

As a last resort there were a number of lines that were taken over and run privately following a rail closure. Usually these were lines run by rail preservationists and steam enthusiasts with little real interest in the transport needs of the area in which the line lay. The services run are largely for tourism and are of little practical transport use. But some lines succeeded in combining preservation and transport goals. One example is the Watchet and Minehead line in Somerset, which runs commuter services throughout the year and eventually hopes to link in with British Rail at Taunton.

The Wareham to Swanage line is another that has been taken over by a preservationist group with aims to provide a transport service. It is not exactly a strategically placed line, but it could be used to aid tourist traffic problems in this area, particularly regarding current proposals for an expensive bypass at Corfe. A parallel could well be drawn between this and the very successful 'park and ride' scheme on the St Erth to St Ives line in Cornwall. This line, also scheduled for closure by Beeching, follows a scenic route along the north Cornish coast parallel to the main road into St Ives. In 1979, as part of a programme to reduce tourist road traffic in St Ives's narrow and congested streets, a new 'park and ride' station was constructed at Lelant Saltings and an improved rail service introduced. The line now carries more passengers than it ever has and St Ives has benefited immensely.

But for each of the successful oppositions to closure there were many lines and stations shut. One such line was the Afan Valley line in South Wales. There is a railway line today that runs from Cardiff up high into the Rhondda Valley, terminating at Treherbert. But prior to 1968 the line carried on past Treherbert to climb to over 1,500 feet above sea level and pass through a tunnel to the Afan Valley and continue from there back to the coast at Bridgend. The hardship arguments for not closing this line were as strong, if not stronger than in the case of the Kyle and Mallaig lines in Scotland. There was only one road link between the valleys, involving a zig-zagging climb up to 1,800 feet before descending down the other side. The rail link was extremely important to the economic, cultural and social life of the two valleys. Thirteen thousand people signed a petition against the closure, but events took on a new complexion when the two-mile tunnel was closed in 1968 when it was declared unsafe for use. The cost of repairs were put at £20–30,000, but nothing was done as a closure notice had been issued for the line as a whole. An emergency bus service ran over the mountains, taking an hour for what was normally a ten-minute rail journey.

In 1969 the public inquiry into the line was held. The objectors' case of hardship was a strong one, but the cost of repairs to the tunnel (which technically should not have been a consideration) were clearly influential. The verdict of the inquiry was to close the line from Treherbert to Bridgend.

The change in government following Harold Wilson leading Labour to power in 1964 made no difference to the rate of rail closures, although once Barbara Castle was appointed as Minister of Transport in 1965 proposals for closure were subject to greater scrutiny. By 1969 nearly 4,000 route miles and hundreds of stations had been axed. Passenger journeys on British Rail had dropped from 1,025 million in 1961 to 805 million in 1969 and freight carried had dropped by 13 per cent. Beeching's plan wasn't working.

Because of the TUCC structure and the emphasis made in the 1962 Transport Act on local hardship being the only basis to oppose rail closure, local protest groups became the main focus for rail closure opposition. There were attempts to counter the whole Beeching approach of closure and retrenchment, but at this scale the power of the road lobby made itself felt. Having effectively taken over the Ministry of Transport and the management of British Railways itself, the forces of the road lobby were in a powerful position to rebuff any national pro-rail counter attack. The railway unions attempted to organise national action through the TUC, but were foiled largely through the power of the Transport and General Workers Union who viewed it to be in their interest that the railways be run down. Equally plans from the unions which would have yielded the required savings without closures were rejected by management. Quite clearly Beeching's *Reshaping* report was the result of powerful vested interests manipulating government and railway management such that the only option they would seriously consider was cuts.

Bus substitution

Where a railway passenger service was cut, the procedure was to replace it with a new bus route, which it was argued could be operated far more economically than a railway line. In practice these replacement bus services experienced considerable problems such that, before long, many came to lose more money than the 'expensive' railway they had replaced!

For example, in their guise as a substitute for the former rail service, the buses attempted to duplicate exactly the routing and scheduling of the railway. No attempt was made to use this as an opportunity to provide improvements, servicing areas just off the rail route or to correct any inherited timetabling faults. Equally, particularly as the majority of the rail lines closed were in rural areas, the replacement bus services had to be operated along often winding and narrow roads, which themselves were prone to congestion at holiday times.

The end result was that passengers by no means found the buses to be an attractive or even viable substitute for the withdrawn trains. Within a few months of the closure of the Bridport to Maiden Newton line in 1975 only one quarter of the ex-rail passengers were using the bus. The bus service was just not as good, convenient and flexible to passengers' needs as the rail services they replaced. The losses of the replacement bus services mounted, such that, even judging Beeching's approach by his own criteria, it became clear that the replacement of bus for rail did not yield net savings to the government.

But what was worse, the replacement bus services could be withdrawn without any legal formality. The law did not require an inquiry for the closure of a bus service as it did for a rail closure. In south-west England alone, 60 per cent of the replacement bus services were withdrawn leaving the areas without any form of public transport at all. Devon lost 78 per cent of its services, Somerset 87 per cent, Gloucestershire 19 per cent and Wiltshire 7 per cent. Any idea that the Beeching Plan would ensure the retention of a viable public transport service for the nation was utterly shattered.

Once a railway was closed, even if circumstances changed dramatically so as to make a reopening viable, it rarely happened. The costs were (and still are) simply prohibitive even if the land were still in railway ownership, as much of it continued to be. This did not only apply to lines which had been completely closed and the track removed, but lines where only passenger services had been withdrawn and trains continued to carry freight. Only one such line has ever had passenger services restored (Barnsley to Penistone in South Yorkshire in 1983).

Even the conversion of the railways to alternative uses has proved difficult. A number of short sections of rail alignments have been used by new roads (one, in south London, aptly named 'The Beeching Cut'!) but schemes to convert extensive amounts of ex-rail lines into roads or busways have proved to be uneconomic in practice. The railway track is generally too narrow, and while it is safe to have trains on rails passing within four

feet of each other at 100 m.p.h., it is by no means safe to have buses or lorries doing so at even half that speed. In 1984 a study into the conversion of old rail lines to road and busway use concluded that all but one of the schemes considered were not economically viable.

The most suitable use for old railways, particularly in urban areas, has been as footpaths and cycleways. Stoke on Trent, in particular, has used its now disused rail tracks to provide a comprehensive network for the cyclist and pedestrian. Such examples to provide a really worthwhile amenity out of the closure of rail lines are unfortunately rare.

The Beeching Report was not really about providing a viable and economic railway system for Britain. A considerably more positive approach of rail investment and development could have done that far more efficiently than Beeching's cuts and retrenchment. Whether Dr Richard Beeching was particularly aware of it or not, he was just a part of a powerful political manipulation intended to reduce the railways to transport insignificance. Beeching considered that his plan would enable the railways to break even by 1970, but even by adopting Beeching's own criteria, his plan was a failure. The cuts and 'rationalisations' had no significant impact on the railways' increasing need for revenue support.

Circumstances that the Beeching Report could never have anticipated certainly contributed to the failure of British Railways to break even by 1970. The decline in the coal and steel industry was undoubtably significant and the assumption of high economic growth (4 per cent per annum) in the economy as a whole certainly knocked Beeching's calculations way out. Economic decline and four million unemployed were not possibilities worthy of consideration in serious economic studies in the 1960s.

34
The Railway Walk, Milton Keynes to Newport Pagnell. The Wolverton to Newport Pagnell branch line was closed under the Beeching Plan in 1964. The remains of the platform of Great Linford station can be seen to the left of this photograph. With the development of Milton Keynes new town in the 1970s this route was used to build a joint footpath/cycleway. Remarkably, this is the third transport use this route has seen. The railway itself was built in 1865 on the line of a branch from the nearby Grand Junction Canal, dating from 1817. (Photo: Stephen Potter)

But although there were external reasons for the Beeching Plan failing to improve the finances of the railways, its greatest weakness was in the overall approach of the *Reshaping* report. It singled out one form of transport, rail, and devised a scheme for that form of transport without recognising the part it played in the nation's transport system as a whole. Furthermore it applied criteria that did not apply to the rest of the transport system, a feature of rail planning that has remained to this day. Finally, its approach was so politically weighted that any methods that did not reduce rail's role were dismissed out of hand. Although couched in glowing terms of 'financial viability' the Beeching Report was, in reality, an axeman's charter.

At around the same time as Mr Marples was giving Dr Beeching the job of surveying the railways with an eye to reducing its scale, Colin Buchanan was also requested to do a transport study, in this case 'to study the long term development of roads and traffic in urban areas.' The Ministry of Transport was worried about traffic congestion, but the findings of the Buchanan Committee pointed to congestion, accidents and car-pollution being an even greater problem than was feared. The implications of Beeching for Buchanan and Buchanan for Beeching were never considered and the two reporting teams went their separate ways.

The beginning of town planning

At the end of the Second World War the nation's housing was attracting more attention than the state of transport services. Pre-war neglect, bombing and a rising population contributed to an acute housing shortage. A series of official reports, both before and during the war, had prompted the view that new housing should be provided as part of an overall town planning process, with land uses more strictly controlled by the state. The post-war Labour government sought to put such ideas into practice with the 1947 Town and Country Planning Act.

The pattern and density of land uses have a major effect on transport demand and as such this act proved to be more influential on urban transport than policies pursued under the heading of 'transport' itself. But the concept of town planning itself had deeper roots and had developed from a reaction against the earlier haphazard growth of Victorian towns and cities.

The story of how our present image of 'town' and 'country' emerged is a fascinating one. Up until the nineteenth century, the predominant image of the city was as a centre of culture and learning. This can be seen in eighteenth-century plays and literature, in which the urban upper classes clearly despised unsophisticated country life. The aristocracy and the rich may have needed their country estates to earn their wealth, but the place for civilised men to be was the city.

The industrial revolution soon changed the image of the city in the eyes of the aristocracy. The belching smoke of the factories, the incoming army of the working classes and the tightly packed slum housing led them to abandon their city houses for their country estates. The up-and-coming industrialists did much the same. The city, so necessary for industrial wealth, became a squalid frightening place.

This 'anti-urban' ideology filtered down the social classes; the country was seen as the antidote to the squalor and cruelty of the town. The dream was to go back and live there yourself. In truth, but for a tiny minority, the squalor was as great, if not greater, in the country. Nineteenth-century rural unemployment and housing conditions were far worse than in the towns. The rural dream was an image of a lifestyle that only existed for a tiny privileged minority.

But it was a dream that had a real influence. If only a minority of dreamers were free to leave the city completely, others could seek a semi-rural existence on the city fringes. But each haven was quickly engulfed

35
A 'Knifeboard' type London horse bus at Kensington, 1891. This was a highly developed version of the horse bus and was the first in London to be fitted with an outside staircase. The dress of the passengers very much reveals the sort of people who used the services.
(Photo: London Regional Transport)

by the houses of other haven-seekers. New developments in transport that seemed to make it possible to live in the country yet work in the city played their role in the massive suburbanisation of Britain's cities that took place from around 1890 to 1939.

Public transport in towns

The nineteenth century saw the beginning of the transport developments that were eventually to enable mass suburbanisation to take place. The first was the horse bus, pioneered in Paris in 1828, imitated in London the following year and copied in other cities during the 1830s. Next came the horse tram, developed in America and first used in Britain in the 1870s. The electric tram, also a product of American initiative, came into service in Britain in the late 1890s. But, initially, the impact of these developments, together with the slowly developing suburban railways, was very selective. Only a minority could afford regularly to travel other than by foot.

Even the largest of the nineteenth-century cities was essentially pedestrian in scale. Walking was the normal means of getting about and quite long distances were covered regularly, particularly by women workers who often had to live nearer to where their menfolk worked. Most towns and cities could be crossed in about an hour by foot, and even London retained a pedestrian scale up until around 1850.

Although the most important form of city transport (which surprisingly it still is to this day), walking could hardly have been pleasant given the vast quantities of horse dung on the ground and the tendency for side streets to be narrow and gloomy. The late nineteenth century saw municipal authorities build new roads and widen existing thoroughfares, but largely these were to accommodate traffic, not people. The boulevards so favoured by French authorities, and which provided very pleasant conditions for the pedestrian, were not a feature of British towns. However, the advantages to pedestrians of the boulevards was little more than a fortuitous byproduct. The first ones, in Paris, were designed this way in order to discourage street rioting and barricade building which was so much easier in the old narrow streets than in the wide boulevards! But before long they did become a more positive concept and were built elsewhere in France for less oppressive reasons.

The horse bus may have been the first true public transport vehicle to see service in our towns and cities, but its impact on city life was very selective. Buses were too expensive for most wage earners and, besides, they hardly increased the scope over what an able-bodied person could do. Their speeds were just too low. Long before there were buses, the middle classes had begun to move to the edge of towns. In these suburbs, the bus became an important feature of life. It was less expensive than the short-distance stage coach and certainly cheaper than hiring a vehicle or keeping a pony and trap. The service extended to the lower middle class the comfort and prestige of riding, but it did not otherwise change their options.

The horse tram was decidedly more efficient than the bus. Being on rails it was able to haul more passengers slightly faster and cheaper. The trams won passengers from the buses and begun to build up a new clientele of a more working-class nature. The horse tram was an important step towards universal public transport.

But of equal importance were the changes that tram operations required in transport organisation. For although trams, like buses, were operated by private companies, the need for fixed track along the roads required much closer co-operation with the municipal authorities. Indeed, in 1870 Parliament passed the Tramways Act to regularise the relationship between local authorities, who were responsible for the roads, and tramway companies who wished to build tracks along them and run tram services.

Glasgow's tramways

The local authority that led the way was Glasgow. The city took an option in the 1870 Tramways Act to build its own track and lease this to a private tram company. Relations with the company were bad and, when the lease expired in 1894, the city decided to take over the business itself. There followed a running battle with the former tramway company which was now operating horse buses in competition with the municipal trams. The company refused to sell its stock, forcing Glasgow to set up its own tram works and become a manufacturer as well as an operator in order that it could run services from the day the lease expired.

The outcome of the struggle between the city and the company was a decisive victory for the city. The old tram company put on an intensive service of horse buses, running some 70 per cent more buses than they had trams. The city responded by cutting trams fares by 50 per cent and within two years had achieved a 60 per cent increase in passenger journeys on its system. The private bus operations slid into obscurity. The venture proved popular in every quarter. Fares had been reduced, conditions of work improved, and the drivers and conductors were given new uniforms as part of a drive to improve the tramway's image. The success was sustained and built on with the electrification of the system in 1899. Furthermore, Glasgow's trams made a profit. Far from being a burden to the rates, municipal tramways subsidised them. By 1917 the tramways had paid off the capital costs of setting them up (which, of course had been abnormally high) and as late as 1938, the trams were still helping to relieve the rates with their profits and were subsidising the loss-making corporation buses.

The electrification of the tramways brought about a revolution in urban transport. Not only were the trams faster, which made longer journeys viable, but electric traction was cheaper than horse power and so fares fell

36
Glasgow trams in the 1950s.
(Photo: Travel Lens Photographic)

rapidly. After the electrification of the Glasgow trams, passenger traffic increased sharply. In 1887 the population of Glasgow averaged 61 rides per head. By 1913 it had risen to 271. In London, over the same period, the number of rides per head rose from 74 to 245. The convenience and pleasure of riding instead of walking was becoming within the reach of almost everyone.

The Glasgow City Corporation positively used trams as a tool of urban policy. They saw electrifying and extending the system as a way of moving people out of Glasgow's notorious slums into better housing at the edge of the city. Previously transport costs ruled out such options for ordinary working-class people. By the 1920s Glasgow's trams were hailed as the cheapest and most frequent tram system in the world. Sixty-three per cent of journeys involved only a halfpenny fare and the city's trams carried more people than all the mainline railways in Scotland!

Tram operations were quite distinct from other methods of public transport. Unlike on buses or trains, women were employed extensively both as conductors and drivers. One woman driver moved to the United States after the Glasgow tramways closed down in order to continue driving trams there. But to continue to work as a driver she had little option. The male dominated unions did not permit women to drive the buses that replaced the trams. In consequence, the demise of trams in Britain threw a lot of women out of work. (Women became bus drivers following the passing of sex discrimination legislation in the 1970s and it was not until 1983 that Anne Winter became the first woman train driver on British Rail.)

37
A 'Coronation' class Glasgow tram on the Mosspark Boulevard reserved track.
(Photo: Travel Lens Photographic)

The fact that Glasgow's trams were profitable was significant in that it encouraged imitation. Running tramways was viewed as a marginal activity for public authorities to engage in. Municipal water, gas, electricity and sewerage were all reasonably acceptable, but despite local authorities' clear responsibility for roads, and the implications that tram tracks had for this, many councils opposed the idea of municipal tram services. Glasgow's popular and profitable experience quelled much political opposition by the expectation that a tramway would prove a money spinner. By 1904, two thirds of the 107 municipal tramways were run by their corporation. The other third involved private companies operating on leased municipally owned tracks. Unfortunately, Glasgow's experience was misleading and the fact that many local authorities acquired tramways with the expectation of making a lot of money out of them had a damaging effect on the long-term development of urban public transport.

London

Public transport development in London was exceptional in Britain, due to the city's size and its commercial and administrative status as the nation's capital. The pressures for urban public transport and for suburbanisation occurred much earlier than elsewhere in Britain and led to a much more complex mix of transport methods. The railways played a far more important part in internal transport than in other cities, with suburban services for middle-class commuters well established by the 1850s. These, together with the earliest underground services on the Metropolitan and District railways, had by the early 1900s encouraged the development of 'dormitory' towns like Croydon, Harrow and Barnet.

The first underground 'tube' line was the City and South London, opened in 1890 between Bank station in the City of London and Stockwell. It now forms part of the Northern Line. It was an electrified line from the very beginning and other 'tube' lines rapidly followed with the Bakerloo, Piccadilly and Hammersmith and Central Lines all being in operation by the First World War. The District and Metropolitan railways electrified their lines from 1903. The eventual development of the tube and subsurface railways, largely north of the Thames, led to London's suburbs extending to eight miles or more from the city centre. The tram network played a considerably smaller part than in other cities, partly because of the well developed and cheap railway network, but also because the City of London Corporation did not permit the tramways through their area. They considered that the overhead wiring would ruin the appearance of the city and that trams catered for an undesirable class of person. So the 'undesirable' classes poured into the City by bus, which remained a relatively more important travel method than in other cities.

Transport in London, by the turn of the century, displayed a rich and varied mixture of methods and ownership. Different parts of London were predominantly served by rail, tube, tram or bus, which encouraged different

sorts of people to live in these areas. South of the Thames was predominantly served by the mainline rail companies that in 1923 became the Southern Railway and took on a prosperous middle-class character. But the inner southern suburbs were tram connected and were of a more working-class nature. To the east of London tramways served a more working-class area around the docks and warehouses. The tubes and the Metropolitan and District served the new suburbs to the north and west. Trams, tubes, buses and railways all attracted further housing development at the edge or a little beyond the built-up area, such that by 1914 London was surrounded by a vast area of what was neither town nor country.

Municipal control came very late to London. Although the London County Council had begun to acquire tramways from the early 1900s, it was not until 1933 that the city's tram, underground and bus services were united. Even then it was incomplete as mainline railways were excluded.

38
Electric trams at Finsbury Park, London, 1930.
(Photo: London Regional Transport)

Garden cities

At the turn of the century there were two major schools of thought about the relationship between transport and urban social welfare. One view was that the existing cities could be considerably improved by resettling the inhabitants of run-down central areas in new estates on the outskirts. Since employment would remain predominantly located where it was, in the centre, improved transport links were an essential precondition of such a stance. As in Glasgow, the introduction of electric trams was seen as a great step forward by many municipalities. 'The modern electric tramway will come to the rescue' was the opinion of a Manchester Housing Committee in 1904. According to an official report of 1905, there was already evidence that 'congested districts have been relieved and that tramways have promoted the development of outlying areas for workmen's and middle class houses.'

The alternative view was considerably more radical, but attracted a lot of support from across the political spectrum such that it eventually became very influential. This was the idea that conventional cities were essentially unsatisfactory for modern society. Improved transport would simply lead to bigger and bigger cities where the inhabitants would not only live in squalid surroundings, but would spend hours travelling in cramped conveyances. The solution was the decentralisation of both people and jobs into smaller settlements, the development of which would eventually lead to the diffusion of the big cities thus creating a new pattern of merged urban/rural settlements.

This 'Garden City' concept of the early 1900s grew from a long history of planned urban developments, the most recent of which had been the

39
London slums. Quite what the Victorian and Edwardian slums were like is hard to envisage today. This photograph only gives a hint of the conditions in which millions of working-class people lived. (Photo: Town and Country Planning Association)

model industrial villages built by philanthropic employers such as Rowntree, Lever and Cadbury. These included Port Sunlight in Cheshire, Bournville, now a suburb of Birmingham, and New Earswick near York. The physical design of these model villages very much influenced the garden cities' founding father, Ebenezer Howard, but his concept of new urban settlements stemmed from a much deeper analysis of what was wrong with the existing city.

There is little doubt that Ebenezer Howard was the inventor of the modern new town. Planned towns on new sites have been built since ancient times, but it was Howard who established the criteria and methods to build new towns in response to urban social and economic problems. He saw the root of these problems as being the very high land values in existing cities which led to overdevelopment, squalid housing conditions and urban poverty. Suburbanisation was just a continuation of this process; to Howard it was no solution. Control and ownership of land he viewed as crucial and so he devised a development process by which community land ownership could come about. This development process was the building of garden cities on new sites well away from existing towns. The land acquired would be cheap and would be held in trust for the garden cities' inhabitants. In the garden city, the people would be their own landlords.

As the garden city developed and land prices rose, the profits would be ploughed back in the form of social welfare services. This would create a new and better urban system. Both factory sites and housing would be cheap, it would have superior social services and the physical environment would be attractive. It was envisaged that if these towns were built in sufficient quantity the land values and rents in existing towns and cities would eventually drop. Given a pattern of declining land values of privately-owned city land and rising values of community-owned garden city land, this would represent a transfer of wealth from city landlords to garden city residents. Eventually, Howard saw landlords being dispossessed peacefully of their property assets, permitting social ownership to become universal. Then existing cities could be redeveloped cheaply and efficiently along garden city lines. The title of his book, *To-morrow: A Peaceful Path to Real Reform*, summed up his approach. It was only later retitled *Garden Cities of To-morrow* in an attempt to popularise the movement.

The role of transport in the design and viability of the garden city was crucial. Howard envisaged garden cities being of a pedestrian scale with a maximum population of only 32,000. In order to provide the facilities and economic attraction of a major city, clusters of these pedestrian-scale towns would be grouped along a railway and tramways to make up a city of 250,000 or more. His theoretical and design concept was well in advance of the embryonic Edwardian planning profession and in practice both the garden cities and subsequent state new towns failed to live up to Howard's design or urban development principles.

Howard helped to establish the two garden cities of Letchworth (founded 1902) and Welwyn (1919). The design of these was in the hands of professional architects and the end result bears only a partial resemblance

40
Garden and social cities. Ebenezer Howard's concept of the development of garden cities was to cluster them into groups, to form a 'social city'. Each individual garden city would then be at a human, pedestrian, scale, while the entire social city (linked by trams and railways) would provide a city-scale level of facilities and life.

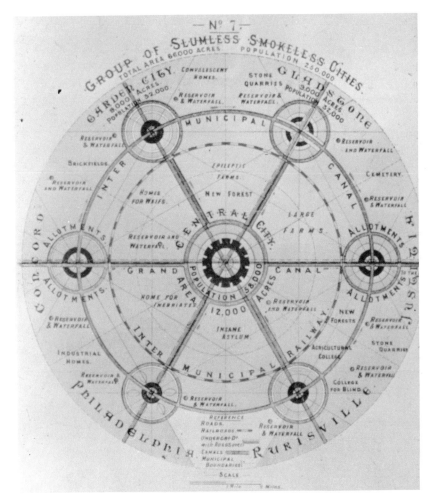

to Howard's radical garden city concept. Letchworth was well located some 35 miles from London with a good rail link to Kings Cross. The town's plan envisaged a pedestrian-scale urban structure and even made provision for a tram link to nearby Baldock, with a segregated track in the centre of Letchworth itself.

Letchworth became famous, but the garden cities movement had changed almost beyond recognition. It had begun as a group of Edwardian radicals, with a clear objective of land reform and a concept of what that could produce. Within a decade this had been transformed into a professional 'town and country planning' organisation whose only objectives seemed to be concerned with the look of the urban environment. The design and construction of garden cities became an objective in itself and their original purpose became totally lost. Even as early as 1904, Thomas Adams, the secretary of the Garden Cities Association, presented the movement's objectives purely in terms of urban design. In the Association's journal he wrote:

41
Letchworth Garden City: the segregated tram route. The 1903 plan for Letchworth included provision for a tram link to Baldock. In the town centre of Letchworth, the trams were to run on a segregated track in the centre of a boulevard. The tramway was never built and the route for it along the Broadway was converted into a pedestrian path. (Photo: Town and Country Planning Association)

'we are becoming better known as an association which stands for design and development as opposed to chance and chaos in urban growth.'

With the emphasis shifting to physical design and the creation of a 'pleasant' environment, planning totally lost its social and economic theoretical roots. It became a profession behind which there was very little thought as to why it did what it did. In consequence, the social and economic ideas that had led Howard to the physical design principles of the garden cities were soon replaced by *ad hoc* aesthetic considerations. The suburbanisation versus garden city stance tended to merge, with 'garden suburbs' being built by private companies together with large planned suburban municipal developments such as Manchester's Wythenshawe.

42
The temporary railway station at Letchworth Garden City. This was hurriedly built in 1905 and served the Garden City until the permanent station was built in 1915. The attitude of the Great Northern Railway towards the development of Letchworth was cautious. The temporary railway station consisted of only a couple of wooden platforms, and a rickety office with a station master who was told that he might be there about three months. Today Letchworth has a population of 35,000. (Photo: Town and Country Planning Association)

Trams in the 20s

The inter-war period also saw vast changes in transport developments themselves. The private car, a plaything of the rich before 1920, was now sufficiently cheap and technically reliable for many of the middle classes to afford. By the outbreak of the Second World War there were around 2 million cars on Britain's roads, double the number a decade earlier.

Ideas about the future of public transport were also fluid. The development of cheap internal combustion engines enhanced the position of the motor bus. In small towns the bus swiftly replaced trams, with the trolly bus representing an interim solution. The big cities, with their extensive tram networks, hesitated and eventually policies diverged. London, Bristol and Manchester, among others, decided to run down their tram operations gradually while other towns, including Glasgow, Leeds and Sheffield, decided to modernise and develop their tramways.

Leeds at the time was a city of nearly half a million inhabitants. Like many industrial cities of inter-war Britain, it had a fairly tight commercial centre surrounded by relatively high density housing and traditional industries with lower density modern estates on the periphery. The residential areas mostly had their own small centres, with shopping and other facilities, and retained a very distinct identity such that a resident would say they came from Headingley or Lawnswood rather than from Leeds.

The city's 70 miles of municipal tramways were arranged in a radial pattern so that lines ran from the outskirts through district centres into the heart of the city; a municipal bus service acted as a feeder for the tramlines or provided crosstown links. One line extended to Wakefield and another connected in with Bradford's tram system.

An example of an area developed in conjunction with a tramway is the council estate of Middleton, on the south of Leeds. This area was built by Leeds City Council in the 1920s to house industrial workers and their families. The council had a programme of buying up the inner city slums and rehousing the inhabitants. This inevitably involved 'overspill' housing at the edge of the city where land was cheap. Middleton was a carefully planned suburb with well designed houses, its own shops and social facilities (even including a cinema), parks and a tram link down to the city where the factories and main shops were.

The tram link was quite exceptional. Leeds was a city that had decided to develop its tramways and the Middleton route looked forward to tramway techniques that were later to be developed in Europe. It largely ran on its own segregated track and at one section the tramline even passed through the park and woodlands. The trams ran at higher speeds and offered a very attractive service to residents. As the Middleton estate developed, so did the tramway, with the last extension being built in 1948–9 to serve a school.

But trams had their disadvantages. The track and overhead wires were relatively expensive to provide and maintain and the cost advantage of electricity over oil was narrowing. The trolly bus represented an attempt

43a (above left)
A tram running through Leeds city centre, 1959
(Photo: Travel Lens Photographic)

43b (above right)
A Leeds tram running on the segregated track at Middleton
(Photo: Travel Lens Photographic)

43c
Leeds tram picks up passengers in Middleton Woods on a misty day
(Photo: Travel Lens Photographic)

to combine the advantages of the motor bus and tram; electrically propelled but without the need to maintain tracks in the road. But the flexibility of the motor bus gave it a considerable advantage and even in towns with extensive tram networks, such as Leeds, passengers often preferred the buses because of their through running and their ability to serve new areas and developments that the tram route missed.

The challenge of the car

But it was among the up and coming car-owning middle classes that the trams faced their final adversary. The attitudes of the 1920s and 30s motorist are best summed up by examining the stance adopted by their motoring organisations at this time. The Royal Automobile Club and the Automobile Association viewed the motorist as a superior class of person,

*A superior class of
person addressing one
of the general multitude*
(Photo: Ford Motor
Company)

and any restrictions on motorists were viewed as sheer affrontery. Hence
the RAC opposed both the introduction of speed limits and the compulsory
driving test. They considered that the skill of the driver was unrelated to
accidents. As to proposals that would provide pedestrians with road crossings at places where the motorist would be expected to stop, this caused a
total outrage. The driver, they considered, should be viewed more highly
than the 'general multitude' and his time as far more valuable. This
despising view of the pedestrian has remained remarkably persistent. In
modern cost-benefit studies, their time is still rated at less than that of the
car driver.

Under these circumstances, it was not surprising that motorists and the
motoring organisations viewed trams and tram tracks as cluttering up the
streets, 'causing' road congestion. This viewpoint met with considerable
sympathy from the equally middle-class municipal authorities and town
planners and very much set the criteria for the modernisation of any tram
system, with proposals for trams in tunnels and on segregated tracks.

45
*The Elephant and
Castle, London, in the
early post-war years.*
Buses and trams which
carried vast numbers of
people came to be
viewed as a traffic
problem by municipal
authorities. The trams
were eliminated and the
traffic problems
multiplied as car use
increased.
(Photo: London
Regional Transport)

By the 1930s the private car and road transport had come to exert a considerable influence upon British urban life. This was not just a matter of inner city road congestion and pollution, but the whole way in which the urban structure of towns and cities was developing. This was particularly so around London and in south-east England. New industrial estates were being located outside existing built-up areas. Most of these only had road access and many of the new suburban housing areas were well away from tram or rail routes. Although cars were available to well under 10 per cent of the population, the effects of car ownership and traffic had a major impact on the layout of many new areas which seriously inhibited public transport operations.

The car and planning

Also by the 1930s, the planning profession was beginning to have a major impact upon new urban developments in Britain. Planning legislation itself was very weak, but via municipal housing developments and the influence of planning thought on private builders' architects, planning ideology was a force to be reckoned with. Road congestion, road safety, pollution and the general impact of mass car use on existing towns and cities was a major concern. This concern was shared by many, including government and municipal authorities. The predominant reaction was very much influenced by American ideas as to how city structures could be adapted to accommodate the car in a safe and environmentally acceptable way.

In America the rise in car ownership and use had been considerably more rapid than in Britain and by the late 1920s this had led to a serious environmental and safety problem. In particular, noise, fumes, accident risk and the general intrusion of traffic into residential areas were all of concern. It was in an attempt to resolve such local environmental conflicts that the American architects Clarence Stein and Henry Wright developed a system of land use and traffic planning that was to bear the name of the obscure new town in which it was first practised: Radburn, in the state of New Jersey.

The basic Radburn idea was to segregate the different functions of roads on to different networks: main through roads would have no built-up frontages; access and local roads in residential areas would be designed so as only to carry the traffic going to or from that area. This would create 'superblocks' or residential islands, free from extraneous traffic. Separate pedestrian and cycle ways would be built, crossing the major roads by underpass or bridges.

So, out of a concern for the problems created by road traffic developed an entire physical planning concept. As with many planning techniques, it found its first application in the post-war new towns programme. These were the direct descendants of Howard's garden city, but their plans portrayed little influence of Howard's careful social and economic considerations of urban design. Most were intended to be of a pedestrian scale, but the splitting up of the towns into neighbourhood 'superblocks', in the Radburn traffic planning tradition, made this difficult. As a result the pedestrian scale was reduced down to these 8,000 population clusters and the restricted facilities that they could offer.

In addition the fragmented pattern of land uses in the new towns, which dispersed traffic flows and so reduced congestion, did exactly the same to public transport demand, making services very difficult to provide as passengers were scattered over a large number of lightly used routes.

46
The plan for Crawley New Town, 1948. The plan for Crawley consisted of a group of 5,000 population neighbourhoods and an industrial estate clustered around the town centre. The road network was basically a traditional radial pattern. This type of urban structure proved difficult to serve by public transport and the neighbourhoods were too small to provide a decent level of facilities within walking distances.

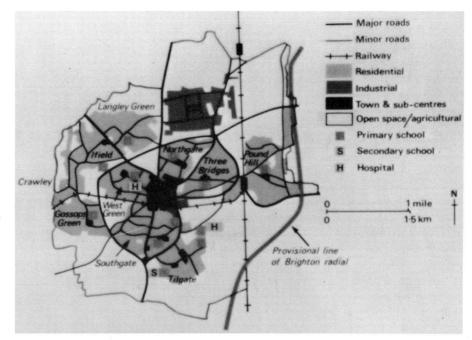

There were one or two new town plans where some attempt was made at real transport and land use planning. In Harlow, Frederick Gibberd clustered four small 5,000 population neighbourhoods together to provide 'districts'. The shopping and social facilities at the district centres were quite large, being supported by 20,000 people, but were within a reasonable walking or cycling distance of even the most remote home. This clustering of neighbourhoods also helped the bus services as demand along main routes was generally good. Unfortunately Gibberd's example was not followed until the mid 1960s new towns of Redditch and Runcorn.

Aycliffe new town, in County Durham, was of a genuinely pedestrian scale, but this was largely a byproduct of the politics surrounding the designation of the town. Unwilling to see too many resources concentrated in one place, the surrounding local authorities succeeded in restricting Aycliffe's population target to only 10,000. This was too small to subdivide into neighbourhoods and so the town was developed as almost a super neighbourhood. The population target was only later increased to 45,000.

The new towns were certainly influential in terms of urban design and, although it was clear that knocking down the existing cities was now a mere dream, the planning methods developed in the new towns led the way for existing urban areas too. The preoccupation in new town plans of providing an urban environment that accommodated road traffic while minimising road traffic's hazards was the theme to follow. The new towns had paid scant attention to the operational needs of public transport; this was not viewed as a problem, whereas car traffic was. The problems that were created in the new towns for public transport took a long time to emerge. The problems of poor pedestrian access were hardly noticed.

Hence when, at the end of the Second World War, Leeds (among other cities) was planning to modernise its tram system by creating more reserved track and putting some routes into tunnels, the whole focus of transport planning had shifted to an entirely different area. There was not the political or professional will to spend millions on upgrading the trams. They were simply scrapped.

The contrast is often made between British and European cities with respect to the use of trams. In many European towns and cities the trams have been developed in such a way that they now form the backbone of the public transport system. Some have been upgraded to form a metro service, as in Vienna, and even relatively small towns can boast extensive tram networks. The contrast between the vigorous development of the tram on the Continent and its total extinction in Britain is often presented as a puzzling paradox. Operational methods and relative prices of oil and electricity are sometimes offered as explanations. But the true cause of the demise of the tram in Britain was ideological and political, not technical.

7 Cars and concrete

Traffic in towns

Just as it seemed that the motorways would solve the problems created by the growth in traffic on inter-urban routes, the roads in towns became a major source of concern. Major cities had always experienced traffic congestion at their very centres and this was almost an accepted part of life. But by the early 1960s traffic congestion, noise, accidents and fumes were becoming part of life in the suburbs and in quite small towns. *Ad hoc* measures like road and junction improvements, and even the much publicised introduction of the parking meter and other restrictions seem to have little effect. In 1961 the Ministry of Transport ordered a major enquiry 'To study the long-term development of roads and traffic in urban areas and their influence on the urban environment.'

It is interesting to note that these terms of reference perceived the problem entirely in terms of the effects of traffic upon the physical environment. There were no transport planning or policy goals set. A steering group under Sir Geoffrey Crowther was set up and a study group, consisting mainly of professional planners, was appointed. The chairman was Colin

47
Traffic congestion in London, 1953
(Photo: Town and Country Planning Association)

Buchanan who was recommended for the job on the basis of his book about the environmental effects of the car, *Mixed Blessing: A Study of the Motor in Britain*.

The resultant report, *Traffic in Towns*, published in the autumn of 1963, very much betrayed the planning heritage of its authors. Given the environmental terms of reference, Buchanan's study group defined their 'problem of design' more precisely as 'to contrive the efficient distribution, or accessibility, of large numbers of vehicles to large numbers of buildings, and to do it in such a way that a satisfactory standard of environment is achieved' (*Traffic in Towns*, p. 40). There was no reference anywhere in the report of the implications this would have for forms of transport other than the private car. When reference to, for example, public transport did occur, this was purely in terms of what role it could play to address environmental traffic problems.

The proposals in *Traffic in Towns* did not represent anything new, but a restatement and development of the 'Radburn' planning principle. Basically, Buchanan's report indicated the ways in which the Radburn planning of new towns could be applied to existing urban areas. The report endorsed the Radburn approach of creating 'environmental areas' within which 'traffic should be subordinated to the environment' and building a hierarchy of roads, including a massive network of urban motorways catering adequately for peak-hour car use at maximum foreseeable levels of ownership.

The report provided examples from a cross section of towns and cities to indicate how plans to cater for peak-hour flows at a 'saturation level' of car ownership could be formulated. These were for Newbury, Norwich, Leeds and the area of central London just to the north of Oxford Street.

Because peak-hour commuting represents the maximum load on a road network, catering for this will provide sufficient capacity for all other uses. Therefore to plan a town's road network requires estimates to be made of the movement from each residential area to the employment zones, translated into numbers of vehicles at a saturation level of car ownership. The use of computers for such traffic models made this complex job a lot easier. It was assumed that all cars available would be used for the work journey and that there would be no restrictions on car use. The basis of this assumption was explained in the report:

> We concluded since it is obviously the desire of society to use the motor
> vehicle to the full, that the only practical basis for a study of the
> present kind was to accept this desire as a starting point and then to
> explore and demonstrate its consequences.

Given a pattern of vehicle flows from homes to workplaces, this movement can then be fitted to a new urban motorway network, the precise lines of which would be determined by local environmental considerations. Any plans for new developments or facilities would have to fit in to this general structure such that they would not put too much pressure on the road

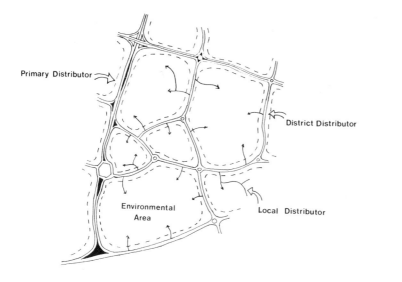

48
A Buchananite urban structure. The ideal modification of towns and cities for mass car use, as considered in *Traffic in Towns*, involved the building of a hierarchy of roads dividing towns up into small 'environmental areas'. Houses, shops, workplaces and other facilities would be served by 'local distributor' roads. These would feed into 'district distributor' roads, which would have no built-up frontages. At the top of the road hierarchy would be the urban motorways, or 'primary distributor' roads.

system at any one point. Generally this favoured a low density, fragmented pattern of urban development.

Within this overall structure, so determined by traffic engineering considerations, would be the 'environmental areas', in which people would live, each up to a maximum of a square mile in size. They could not be any larger as this would impose too great a strain on the motorway network and would also generate sufficient traffic within the area to cause problems. Within such areas, *Traffic in Towns* suggested the development of segregated footpaths and cycleways for local movement and the use of a pattern of distributor and estate roads so as to discourage through traffic.

49
Oxford Street, London. Buchanan showed that the whole area would have to be demolished and rebuilt in order to cope with all the people who work and shop here travelling by car.

50
Hydraulic car parking, Washington DC. The cost of land in city centre areas is such that very expensive forms of car parking are necessary. This is, perhaps, a rather exceptional example, where cars are jacked up on hydraulic lifts to allow others to park underneath.
(Photo: Stephen Potter)

Although viewed as an ideal, Buchanan recognised that in many situations such 'full motorisation' would not be possible for reasons of cost or environmental damage. The design for a fully motorised Oxford Street required the virtual demolition of the whole of this area in order to provide sufficient room for roads and car parking for the large number of journeys to and from this part of central London. Only the odd 'historic' square remained as pedestrians and cars were segregated on to different levels. For any city over about 300,000 such problems would occur. Another case where full motorisation could not be achieved was in an historic city; Norwich was the example used by Buchanan. In both these examples some measure of restraint would be needed on car use and the promotion of public transport was advocated as one possible supplementary tool to highway engineering. No suggestions, however, were provided as to *how* this could be achieved.

In the vast majority of situations Buchanan considered that full motorisation planning was possible and desirable. It would require an enormous amount of public expenditure to adapt Britain gradually to mass car use, but this was considered as entirely justified.

Traffic in Towns proved to be very influential, not so much because what it said was new, but because the ideas in it were presented in a coherent form, were backed up by practical studies of real places, and offered a clear and simple answer to a major problem. In 1964 the government issued a circular advising local authorities to produce plans consistent with the findings of *Traffic in Towns*, which resulted in revised county development plans based on Buchanan's traffic and land use planning techniques. Planning had become a branch of traffic engineering.

North Bucks New City and Milton Keynes

The techniques developed in *Traffic in Towns* purely related to providing a massive amount of roadspace in an environmentally acceptable way. It was by no means a transport planning document as non-car travel was

89

involved, if at all, in a purely incidental capacity. It made no reference to transport planning objectives or to the conflicts that occur in the urban design for different forms of transport. However, there have been a number of attempts at incorporating transport planning into a Buchanan-style urban design exercise. One, which was almost exactly contemporary with *Traffic in Towns*, was a plan for a North Bucks New City on the site that is now occupied by the new town of Milton Keynes.

The one feature of the North Bucks New City plan that is always mentioned is its use of a monorail as the main passenger transport system. Although various types of monorails have been around since the 1890s, the 1960s saw a spate of monorail plans and experimental tracks, together with considerably more innovative public transport systems.

But the inclusion of a monorail in the North Bucks plan did not just represent an application for innovative technology; it indicated a clear departure from the Buchananite preoccupation with road networks and a move towards the development of a transport planning approach to urban design. The basic structure of the North Bucks New City was almost a modern adaptation of Ebenezer Howard's Social City. It consisted of a double looped monorail track linking a series of pedestrian-scale settlements. The main road network was kept to the periphery of the city. It was envisaged that the monorail service could be provided free of charge (funded by the rates), and as such would reduce demand for roadspace to such an extent that only a small, inexpensive, network would be needed. There would be no restriction on car use, but a free public transport service would be provided.

The design was intended to provide access for all, not just for cars as Buchanan had redefined the word 'access' to mean. It would provide an urban structure which, by locating transport-generating land uses along the public transport route, gave public transport a competitive edge, rather than decimating it, which is what a Buchanan-type urban structure does. It was a design which permitted each form of transport to do what it was best at. Pedestrian and cycle access was good for short journeys, public transport catered for mass flows, and the private car for journeys which public transport or walking could not adequately serve. To the individual it meant a high quality of transport service however they chose to travel.

But North Bucks New City was never built. It was too large a project for Bucks County Council, whose planners had designed it, to tackle alone. They required government funds. A political wrangle ensued as to who would have control over the project and whether it should be primarily for the housing needs of Buckinghamshire or as a overspill new town for London. In the end, Milton Keynes was designated as a government-run, London overspill, new town. In order to distance themselves from the North Bucks New City scheme, the government-run development corporation commissioned a separate plan. The ultra-Buchananite *Plan for Milton Keynes* (Llewelyn-Davies *et al.*, 1970) was the result.

The plan for the new town of Milton Keynes was carefully designed to provide for the highest levels of car use whilst maintaining a variety of

51

The plan for Milton Keynes, 1970. The existing towns of Bletchley, Wolverton and Stony Stratford were planned to be linked by a mesh of dual carriageway 'grid' roads serving a dispersed, low-density, pattern of urban development. The original population target for the new town was 250,000, although this was subsequently lowered to 180,000. This is expected to be reached by 1990.

52

Los Angeles. The design of Milton Keynes was a purposeful imitation of Los Angeles; 'a modified Los Angeles system' was how Milton Keynes designer, Lord Llewelyn-Davies, described it.

environmental goals that were also very much in vogue in the 1960s. This proposed a very low density, fragmented town so as to spread traffic on roads over as wide an area as was possible and in as even a fashion as was possible. Housing was planned at 28 persons per acre with an overall population density of 11 p.p.a., the lowest of any new town and at least half the density of most suburban areas. With a reduction in the town's population target, overall densities are now down to 9 p.p.a. To complement this land use pattern, a 'grid' of dual carriageway roads some 1 km apart was proposed, flanked by 100-yard-wide landscaping 'buffers' of earth ramparts and trees to shield residential areas from noise and fumes.

Although the published plans referred to the need for a high quality public transport service, with mini-buses running every three to five minutes, tucked away in the *Transportation Technical Supplement* (vol. 2, p. 34) was the confession that 'in the light of the selected land use plan, the provision of a competitive form of public transport does not make practical sense. This consideration of freedom of choice [between travel methods] has therefore been discounted' and 'the appropriateness of providing a public transport service beyond the minimum level necessary . . . is solely a matter of policy.' Or, to dejargonise it, 'the design of Milton Keynes can't support a decent bus service, so we've abandoned that as an objective. If you do want a decent bus service you'll just have to subsidise it a lot.'

While stating the need for a good public transport service in one volume of the town's plan, the designers of Milton Keynes admitted that their Buchananite design could not fulfil this objective. Rather than change their cherished plan, they dropped the goal for a high quality public transport service.

Construction of Milton Keynes began in 1970 and now 110,000 people live there, with a further 70,000 planned to move in by 1990. Economically, the town has been very successful, especially given the recession of the 1980s, but the one major headache in Milton Keynes development has been transport. It has been necessary to spend well over £100 million on grid and trunk roads and the officially 'temporary' need for large bus subsidies has grown rather than diminished. By the early 1980s it became clear that a policy of substantial subsidies would not just be needed to maintain a high quality public transport service, but any public transport at all. In 1982–3 subsidies totalling £997,000 (42 per cent of running costs) kept a basic bus service (11 routes, 30-minute frequency) in operation.

In the mid-1970s, there was an experiment with Dial-a-Bus (a kind of shared taxi), in the hope that a technological answer could be found to the hostile operational environment of Milton Keynes. These buses made a larger loss than conventional services and were all withdrawn by 1980. The focus has shifted from planning and technology to the promotion of existing services and endeavouring to find politically acceptable ways of maintaining high subsidies. Most of the present subsidies come from the development corporation, and with its gradual winding down and eventual demise by 1990, the future of public transport services in Milton Keynes looks bleak.

This experience very much identifies the weakness of Buchanan's approach. The objectives that were set in *Traffic in Towns* to provide a physical environment which could cope with the problems of noise, pollution and congestion were entirely laudable. But this is only one aspect of the problems created by mass car use. Such an environmental planning approach can only work if it is part of an overall transport planning process. If it is not, then it creates far more problems than it can solve simply because this traffic engineering approach cannot identify the social and economic consequences of its actions.

Transport planning, in the true sense of the word, is a rarity in Britain. But it is not unknown. Two examples from among the new towns are the plans for Redditch and Runcorn.

The campaign for real transport planning

Arthur Ling, the designer of Runcorn, realised that Buchanan's methods had to be applied within a planning context that recognised the inherent conflicts in the operational conditions for different types of transport. In addition he did not share Buchanan's view that massive resources would be made available to transform totally our towns and cities for saturation car use and to tidy up all the social and economic problems that this would create. Although he accepted that mass car ownership was here to stay, he considered that wider criteria should be used in planning than just protecting people from traffic noise and fumes:

> To design the town [i.e. Runcorn] dominantly for the motor car would require the maximum expenditure on highways to cater for peak-period traffic and a more extensive provision of car parking spaces at the Town Centre and in the industrial areas. In addition, public transport . . . would be little used and therefore it would be uneconomic to operate a frequent service. This would cause a sense of social isolation

93

for those without the use of a car, such as children and old people, and also members of the family to whom the car is not available at a particular time. (Arthur Ling, *Runcorn New Town*, 1967)

It is interesting to compare this with the more recent writings of the French urban sociologist Manuel Castells:

This extreme dependence on the automobile creates new sources of discrimination – all non drivers are seen as virtually handicapped. Such is the case for the aged, for adolescents, for housewives when the husband has gone to work in the car, for the sick but also for the great segment of the population not equipped with a car . . . so many immobile people destined to consume little else but television. So many 'living dead'. (Manuel Castells, *City, Class and Power*, 1978)

Both authors, from very differing viewpoints, express the same concern; that the car can never be a universal form of transport, but is sufficiently widespread to erode the operational environment of other forms of transport, especially if planners make that a design goal.

The plan for Redditch, designed by Hugh Wilson and Lewis Womersley in 1966, also followed this line of thinking. It accepted the existence of mass car use, but saw the real challenge not as being to design an urban structure that could accommodate high car use, but one that could, under conditions of high car ownership, provide a good public transport service too. One of their design goals was specifically the requirement to produce an urban form capable of supporting a high quality bus service. It is interesting to note that they did not view themselves in conflict with *Traffic in Towns* but to be developing the need that Buchanan had identified for techniques to promote public transport.

The designs of Runcorn and Redditch are very similar. The towns are quite small (their target populations were both around 100,000, although these have now been reduced) and so buses were used rather than trains, monorails or trams. Bus and car flows are on *separate* networks, with the size of residential areas being determined by the number of people necessary to support a frequent bus service. Facilities are primarily located along the bus routes. In both towns, but particularly in Runcorn, there are substantial sections of bus-only roads (Busways), for by segregating bus routes from the main roads it becomes possible to concentrate public transport flows to encourage a good service while dispersing car flows to eradicate congestion.

Both towns do have a rail service for long-distance services, Runcorn's being far better as it is on the main Liverpool to London line, whereas Redditch is at the end of a branch line from Birmingham. Recently a new station has opened at Runcorn on the local line from Chester to Manchester.

The construction of Runcorn and Redditch is now essentially complete and in practice these towns have shown that real transport planning can do a considerable amount to address the design and operational conflicts

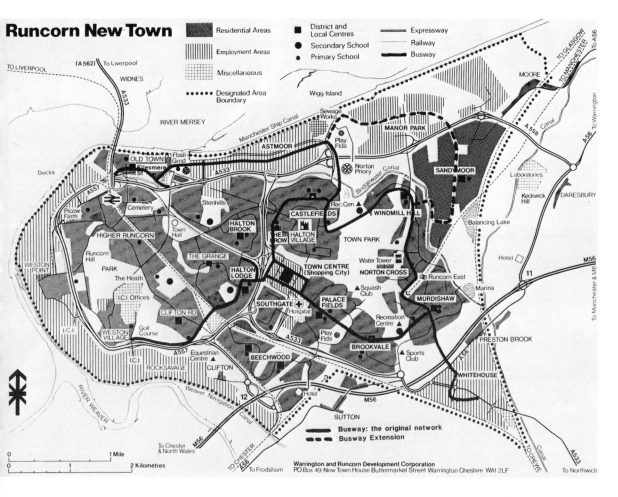

Runcorn New Town

▬ Residential Areas	■ District and Local Centres
▦ Employment Areas	● Secondary School
▦ Miscellaneous	• Primary School
•••• Designated Area Boundary	— Expressway
	⋯ Railway
	━ Busway

— Busway: the original network
▪▪▪ Busway Extension

Warrington and Runcorn Development Corporation
PO Box 49 New Town House Buttermarket Street Warrington Cheshire WA1 2LF

54
The plan for Runcorn New Town, 1967. The existing town of Runcorn is to the left. New residential and employment areas were built around the busway with main roads to the periphery of the town. This has proved to be an economical design to build and provides well for both public transport and the car user.

between private and public transport. This achievement is particularly of note as it relates to relatively small towns where public transport operations are usually less viable than in cities.

In Runcorn a service frequency of 5 to 10 minutes is in operation and in Redditch a 10-minute frequency has been achieved. However, what is of particular note is that these public transport systems require very little subsidy. In Redditch 6 per cent of operating costs are subsidies and about 5 per cent in Runcorn. These are all considerably lower than the 42 per cent subsidy in Milton Keynes for a 30-minute frequency bus service. Problems have occurred regarding the quality of the bus services as opposed to their frequency and, in Redditch in particular, the fares are not exceptionally cheap.

In addition, the road networks of Redditch and Runcorn have proved to be of ample capacity with no restrictions on car use. The Busways of the two towns have not succeeded in attracting as many car users as was envisaged, but they still succeed in providing a high quality service all the same.

55
The Runcorn Busway at Castlefields. Among most of its length, the Busway is treated much like a railway, being fenced off and crossed by pedestrian underpasses and road bridges.
(Photo: Warrington and Runcorn Development Corporation)

56
The Runcorn Busway in the Town Centre. The Busway here is elevated so as to be at the same level as the first floor shopping centre to the right of the picture.
(Photo: Warrington and Runcorn Development Corporation)

This design has also succeeded in enhancing pedestrian accessibility, as the large catchments to the public transport routes succeed in supporting more local facilities than usual. So to a large extent, urban designs that are conducive to a good quality public transport service enhance pedestrian and cycle access too. But local physical conflicts with traffic need to be recognised in the provision of road crossings and separate foot and cycle paths. Indeed, in terms of the more recent preoccupation of energy conservation, the effect of such designs on pedestrian access is more significant than the provision of good public transport services. A slight modification of the Runcorn/Redditch design to provide larger catchments to local facilities can make upwards of 60 per cent of journeys within walking distance of the home, compared to only 30 per cent in a dispersed Milton Keynes-type urban structure. This elimination of the need for motorised travel could cut energy use by up to a third.

Table 3   Key characteristics of the new towns examined

	Milton Keynes	Washing-ton	Redditch	Runcorn	Peter-borough
Population	107,000	55,000	68,000	65,000	124,000
Current gross density, p.p.ha	12	24	23	22	19
Planned gross density, p.p.ha	20	27	25	34	23
Development costs to state per person housed	£10,200	£11,000	£4,100	c.£7,000	£5,300
Average bus frequency	30min.	20min.	10min.	5min.	15min.
Cost of bus season ticket per week	£2.40	£1.65	£3.50	£2.50	£3.50
Subsidy as % of bus running costs	42	n.a.	6	5	14
Av. no. of shops at local centre	5	9	15	7	23

Note: This table includes two extra new towns to those considered in the text. Washington (in north-east England) is of comparable size to Redditch and Runcorn, but designed similarly to Milton Keynes. Peterborough is comparable in size to Milton Keynes but designed in order to promote public transport. Sources of data: Steadman, 1983 and Potter, 1984.

Planning for transport

The new towns have always pioneered planning techniques and outside them there are few really major examples of attempts to implement either Buchanan's urban traffic engineering concept or co-ordinated land use/

57
The pedestrianised town centre, Stevenage
(Photo: Stevenage Development Corporation)

transport planning. Elements of both seem to crop up at certain times and in certain places. Public transport priority has tended to mean little more than bus lanes. There have been no real attempts in existing areas to create a separate busway system to the roads and to incorporate route catchments into the planning process.

More effort has gone into environmental improvements in town centres, largely due to the damage and inconvenience inflicted by traffic. The creation of pedestrianised areas, especially in historic cities, has greatly improved the environment of the streets. It has often helped to invigorate a shopping area declining due to poor pedestrian access, noise and traffic fumes. Fully pedestrianised shopping centres, pioneered at Coventry and Stevenage in the 1950s, are now commonplace. But the degree to which we in Britain pedestrianise our city centres is meagre compared to many European countries. This involves the pedestrianisation of the whole of many city centres compared to schemes for a few streets at most in British towns and cities.

58
'Pedestrianised' street in York. Vehicles are allowed for 'access only', the result of which is a far from pedestrianised 'environmental area'.
(Photo: Stephen Potter)

59
Model of the multi-level town centre, Cumbernauld. This was designed at the same time as Buchanan was working on *Traffic in Towns*. Roads and car parking occupied the ground level with shopping and commercial facilities on the first floor and expensive penthouses above. In practice this design has not been popular; the penthouses are no longer in use and modern-day shopping developments have veered away from such expensive and architectural multi-level designs.

But although pedestrianisation may create a pleasant environment for the particular streets that are returned to the people, unless this is combined with other transport planning measures it hardly does much more than shift the misery and danger of traffic to another part of the town.

Buchanan's idea for multi-level redevelopment, where traffic flows are likely to be very high, are rare. The Barbican, in the City of London, is the closest to his concept. This was begun just before the *Traffic in Towns* study team undertook their work and was not sufficiently advanced in 1963 for them to evaluate it. Cumbernauld new town centre, the first part of which opened in 1966, was also designed on a multi-level principle. Few big cities have attempted a full-scale Buchananite reconstruction, but Leeds did

60
Leeds Inner Ring Road. This motorway-type road loops around the city centre of Leeds, passing into a tunnel at one point and occasionally being crossed by pedestrian footbridges.
(Photo: Stephen Potter)

evolve a plan for the central area which in many respects followed the principles of *Traffic in Towns*.

In fact, the most widespread reaction to *Traffic in Towns* was to implement elements which appealed to local authorities or their highway and planning departments, and to disregard the rest. Major road schemes had considerable political support (as was discussed with respect to 'the road lobby' in Chapter 4) and now had cash backing from central government. Pedestrianisation got some money and enthusiasm as well, but the concept of developing separate pedestrian and cycle networks was utterly ignored, despite it being the cheapest element of the Buchanan package. Buchanan's undeveloped loose end of promoting public transport, although well developed in new town urban theory and practice, received little attention or understanding elsewhere until the mid-1970s.

The whole concept of 'environmental areas' never really took off. New roads were built, which in Buchanan's scheme had the dual purpose of achieving environmental improvements as well as catering for traffic growth. The former was soon forgotten, or rather, disregarded. The linking of new road construction to planning was always tentative; once the highway engineers got the resources to build roads the ethos of 'roads for road users' predominated and many of the environmental benefits that could have accrued from new road construction were lost through sheer indifference.

The biggest obstacle to the whole idea of restructuring towns and cities to cope with 'full motorisation' in a Buchanan-style scheme proved to be cost. The railways may have underestimated the costs of their 1950s modernisation plan by 10 per cent or so, but Buchanan's optimism for the availability of billions of pounds to rebuild much of urban Britain was of a totally different order of magnitude. Despite this, the concept of 'full motorisation' highway engineering was popular and, although never fully implemented anywhere outside the new towns, *Traffic in Towns* stimulated the construction of thousands of miles of new, widened or improved roads. Such attitudes gave little encouragement to the planners to develop real transport planning, in the true sense of the word, as it had been at Runcorn and Redditch. With highway engineers forging ahead with well financed road projects, little thought was given to the relationship between urban development and the public transport network. All attention was focused on planning for the car.

Even in relatively minor matters, there seemed to be no link between urban development plans and public transport provision. Aycliffe new town, near Newcastle upon Tyne, had to wait until 1977 for the railway station that was included in its 1948 Master Plan. It was not as if the line that ran past the town did not already carry a passenger service. For nearly thirty years the passenger trains trundled past Aycliffe without stopping.

Corby, too, is a case worth examining as it had an existing service that was withdrawn just as plans for further expansion were announced. Corby, a steel works town, was designated a new town in 1950. At that time it had a population of 15,700 people and the purpose of the new town desig-

61
Milton Keynes Central Station. Unlike Aycliffe, Milton Keynes secured a new town centre station relatively quickly. This was opened in 1982, three years after the shopping centre began trading and while office blocks were still being built around it. (Photo: Stephen Potter)

nation was to diversify its economic base to provide jobs for women as well as to build houses. It was planned to increase Corby's population to 45,000. Corby was served by a branch line from Kettering (on the main London to Sheffield line), which acted both as a freight link to the steelworks and provided a passenger service for the town. By the 1960s there was already some concern as to the future of steelmaking in Corby and plans were laid to attract a far wider range of industry as part of a major expansion of the town from its old 45,000 population target to 80,000. Corby's transport links were seen as a vital part in attracting new firms. The expansion plan was announced in 1966.

But the passenger rail service to Corby was due for closure under the Beeching Plan. That Corby was growing and was planned to grow at an even faster rate seemed to make no difference to the decision. The line closed in the same year as Corby's expansion was announced. Employment in the steelworks ran down and, in 1980, steel making ceased in Corby altogether. Male unemployment reached nearly 30 per cent and the town now has an Enterprise Zone and regional grants that are more a characteristic of northern England than of Northamptonshire.

The freight line is actually more important now as it brings in steel made at Scunthorpe for finishing at Corby. Yet there is still no passenger service. Plans to reopen the line have been mooted and it is suggested that this would be the key to some employment-generating projects. But without a passenger service Corby looks like remaining a rather remote location in the eyes of most industrialists.

Transport planning is a rare and endangered species in Britain. The ability exists to provide urban structures capable of reconciling, or at least minimising, the conflict between private transport, the pedestrian and public transport, but there does not seem to be any sign of the slightest interest in such an objective. Compared to the real political, industrial and economic power that highway engineering and the motor industry has, planning is a political weakling and it is in the interest of too many powerful people that it should remain so.

8 Capital city

SPEED
LIMIT
4
M.P.H.

PRIVATE

KGU 292

KYY 824

The decline of London Transport

In the 1940s London could boast that it had the largest underground railway system in the world, providing an exceptionally high standard of service and comfort. Indeed London had pioneered underground railways, with the opening of the Metropolitan Railway from Paddington to Farringdon in 1863. Throughout the nineteenth century this system had developed, first with the sub-surface lines like the Metropolitan and District, and then from the 1890s with the deep-level tubes. The latter developed rapidly and most of the tube network as we now know it was completed by 1907. From 1926 the only major addition up to the late 1940s was the extension of the Central Line east from Liverpool Street to take over the British Rail line to Hainault and Epping.

Despite the size of the underground network, developments had fallen

62
Queuing for the tube at Oxford Street in the early 1950s
(Photo: Town and Country Planning Association)

63
A Piccadilly Line train entering Hammersmith station. This is on the route to Heathrow Airport.
(Photo: Stephen Potter)

far behind the growth of London. The war obviously held things up, but the effects were to some extent offset by increased passenger usage. After the war the service recovered quickly, largely thanks to the perceptive and talented management team at the London Passenger Transport Board. By 1948, public transport in London was carrying an all-time peak of nearly 5,000,000,000 passengers a year. But this recovery was short-lived.

From the mid-1950s public transport use declined steadily year after year. Certainly the population of London itself was declining. From 1951 to 1979, the population of Greater London fell from 8 million people to under 7 million. By the 1981 Census, its population had dropped to 6.7 million. In Inner London the fall was even more marked, from 3.3 million to 2.4 million from 1951 to 1979, a decline of 27 per cent.

But this outward movement of people did not explain the decline in tube and bus travel. The majority of the movement was to places within commuting distance of the city. People still worked in London and required the bus or underground as part of their commuting journey. Also there were factors which should have *increased* public transport use, such as the development of tourism and, from 1977, the short extension of the Piccadilly Line to Heathrow Airport. The growth of tourism in particular has a large impact on public transport use as most tourists do not have the use of a car. Numbers of foreign visitors to London grew steadily throughout the 1950s and 70s to top 6 million in 1972. By 1977 the figure was almost 8 million.

Yet public transport use in London continued to decline. The main factor was simply the growth in car ownership. This particularly affected the buses, both in terms of patronage and their operating conditions. The number of private cars entering central London during the morning peak rose from 75,000 in 1962 to 129,800 in 1978. Between 1955 and 1965, a crucial decade when the economy of bus operations was undermined, the number of private cars heading for central London in the morning peak rose by 28,800. These additional vehicles occupied more than five times the amount of roadspace vacated by the 1,900 fewer buses, which had been partly driven off the roads by traffic congestion.

The financial difficulties that London Transport faced in the 1950s and 60s mirrored those in the urban bus industry as a whole. However the sheer scale of London Transport operations resulted in a crisis point being reached earlier. 'Inadequate resources' was the term most often used by London Transport management when listing their problems. The expectation was that the system would generate its own resources and at that time no regular support was provided by the public purse. But with congestion (over which LT had no control) pushing up costs and passenger numbers decreasing, a situation had been created of external factors determining the economic environment in which bus services operated. Maintaining and operating services was borne mainly by passengers; the only way additional revenue could be raised was by putting up fares and this proved to be totally self-defeating. One 12 per cent fare increase in the 1950s resulted in an immediate loss of 60 per cent of bus passengers. Although most eventually returned, there was a permanent loss of 16 per cent, enough to wipe out the proceeds from the fares increase. This pattern was to be repeated over and over again until the coming of 'Fares Fair' in 1981.

These financial constraints had their implications right down to the day-to-day running of London Transport services. In particular, obtaining an adequate supply of reliable labour for relatively low-paid jobs involving unsocial hours in London Transport proved to be a headache for LT's management throughout the three decades 1950 to 1980. During this period, unemployment was consistently lower in London than the national average, so full employment combined with low wages and the unsocial hours that public transport operations demand resulted in a constant labour shortage. In addition the unions would not agree to the employment of women as train or bus drivers – this was viewed as a threat to male jobs.

In 1955–6 the labour shortage reached a crisis point and recruitment in the West Indies was undertaken. Initially seventy station men and twenty women bus conductors were engaged and given an interest-free loan from the British government for fares from Barbados, repayable by monthly instalments.

British Rail were also short of staff, for much the same reasons, and went recruiting both to the West Indies and to Ireland. The effect that these recruitment programmes had on encouraging immigration from the West Indies to Britain is probably one of the less emphasised aspects of British transport policy in the 1950s. Immigrant labour could only be a short-term solution. To maintain an adequate and stable workforce, more attractive wages were needed and this brought management back to the overwhelming problem of insufficient resources to maintain and develop London's public transport system.

The Victoria Line and the Motorway Box

Following the Second World War there had been a number of plans for the development of London and for investment in new rail and tube lines. A report in 1949 recommended the construction of eight new passenger lines, totalling 97 route miles and a special freight line of 5.5 miles. This was simply in order for the rail system to catch up with the growth of London that had occurred. It was recognised that such a scheme would have to be funded from the public purse and, in principle, public investment for such capital projects was politically acceptable. But, in practice, the sums proved too large for the Treasury to accept and only one of these routes, the Victoria Line, was built. The go-ahead for that was delayed until 1962.

It was not only new tube lines that were planned in the 1940s, but the closer integration and joint development of London Transport and British Railways services. A foretaste of this were the pre-nationalisation schemes whereby the Northern Line was extended to join and take over LNER track to High Barnet and the similar scheme whereby the Central Line was linked to the LNER suburban line out of Liverpool Street to Epping and Ongar. Both of these were completed just after the war. But the breaking up of the British Transport Commission in 1953 with the total demise of

64
A train entering Seven Sisters station on the Victoria Line
(Photo: London Regional Transport)

any government support for the transport co-ordinating role that it had fulfilled, meant that further plans to integrate London Transport and British Rail services and for the rationalisation of track had little chance of success. It was hoped that the Victoria Line project would facilitate integration, given that it now provided seven stations common to both London Transport and British Rail. In practice progress on British Rail/ London Transport integration did improve, but its effects were selective. In particular, the Highbury branch of the Northern Line was transferred to British Rail as part of a project to electrify its suburban services into Moorgate from Welwyn Garden City and Hertford. However, the fares charged by the two remained entirely separate and progress towards the integration of services and facilities was slow.

Just as British Rail financing suffered from the rise to power of road interests within national government, so too did London Transport. Money was not so tight when it came to funding new roads. In 1959 the Roads Campaign Council ran a 'New Ways for London' competition for the best design of a long-term plan for highway development in the city. Colin Buchanan was one of the panel judges that awarded the first prize to J. A. Proudlove's 'A Traffic Plan for London'.

Proudlove noted that while road traffic was growing in Britain as a whole at a rate of 14 per cent per annum, in London the annual growth rate was only 2 per cent. The relatively slow growth of traffic in London was seen as the real problem to be solved:

> The present slow increase in traffic will be hastened as changes take place which presently maintain this unnaturally low figure. Namely the lack of road and parking space and the effective public transport system able to operate at rates cheaper than private travel.

Note that a cheap, effective public transport system was considered undesirable.

Proudlove's prize-winning scheme, though not acted upon, provided the guiding principles for some of the major London traffic studies which were subsequently incorporated into the 1971 Greater London Development Plan. This plan was produced by the Greater London Council which had been formed in 1965 by combining the old London County Council with the county of Middlesex and parts of the counties of Essex, Kent and Surrey.

The problems of traffic management were an important reason behind the creation of the Greater London Council. London's road network, most of which was established before the invention of the car, came under increasing strain during the 1950s and early 1960s. The construction of the North Circular Road and a number of new radial 'arterial' roads had made little difference and the movement of population out of London County into Middlesex, Essex, Surrey and Kent resulted in vast flows of traffic across administrative boundaries laid down in a less mobile era. The different local traffic authorities found themselves vainly trying to cope with growing traffic, of which an increasing proportion was just passing through their areas.

One of the first acts of the newly created Greater London Council was the announcement of plans to build the 'Motorway Box'. This plan was extraordinarily ambitious, envisaging the construction of an inner ring road close to the congested, densely built-up centre of London on very high-value land. When first presented it was estimated to cost £25,000,000 per mile, taking 6,000 acres of some of the most expensive land in Britain and would have involved the destruction (and rebuilding elsewhere) of houses occupied by 100,000 people, equivalent to nearly two new towns the size of Harlow or Stevenage. Its costs would have swamped that of all other major projects under way at the time, including Concorde, the Channel Tunnel and the Third London Airport. And this was at the same time that London Transport was being forced to recruit cheap labour from abroad because it could not pay higher wages for its staff.

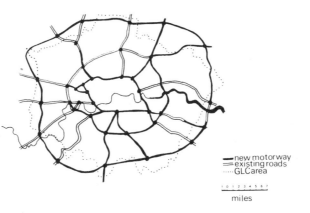

55
The Motorway Box. The 1969 plan for the three London Ringways involved both building new motorways and upgrading existing routes, like the North Circular Road, to motorway standards. The outer Ringway has been built as the M25 but the inner Ringways 1 and 2 were abandoned.

new motorway
existing roads
GLC area

miles

The plans for the Motorway Box provoked fierce controversy and became one of the focal issues of the 1973 GLC elections. As an appreciation of the disruptive implications of the plans grew, especially in the path and alongside the proposed new motorways, opposition began to get organised. It was the Labour Party within the GLC who had initially proposed the Motorway Box, but the torrent of complaints from residents in the inner London areas through which the motorways were due to go soon changed the Labour Party's mind. The inner Motorway Box was due to pass almost exclusively through Labour-held territory. The result was that in the 1973 GLC elections, Labour campaigned against the Motorway Box and won.

The new Labour-controlled GLC largely abandoned road building within the capital in favour of a policy of restraining car traffic and promoting public transport. However they considered that the outer ring road of the Motorway Box (later to become the M25) should be built in order to divert through traffic, particularly lorries, away from central London. In its *Transport Policies and Programme 1977–82*, published in 1976, the council spelt out the transport objectives of this change in direction. It was the intention that peak-hour traffic levels in central London be reduced to two thirds of their 1974 level.

London takes on London Transport

At this time of debate over the spending of vast sums on an urban motorway system for London, the downward spiral of public transport use was continuing. In 1971 a fares increase on London Transport succeeded in bringing out the protesters. A decade later, passenger journeys by public transport in London were lower than at any time since 1912. Bus journeys were consistently slower than in the 1920s and fares were almost the highest of any major city in Europe. Policies to improve roads were easy to implement and were permanently effective. Policies to improve public transport proved to be fraught with delays and half-hearted commitments and so were easily reversed.

A major step forward was the Transport London Act of 1969, which brought about the most far-reaching changes to transport in London since the creation of London Transport in 1933. This Act set up the London Transport Executive (LTE) to take the place of the London Transport Board. But the really important feature of the Act was that overall control of the new undertaking was given to the Greater London Council, which had the duty of laying down 'principles' of transport operation and of giving 'general directions' to the new Executive. With London Transport added to its road building responsibilities, the GLC was now in a position to implement effective overall transport planning in the capital. What happened in practice was that the London Transport Executive had to alter its priorities

66
Buses held up in the London traffic and by illegal parking
(Photo: Stephen Potter)

with each major change in fortunes of the two main political parties at County Hall. Transport became a left–right political issue and it was the public transport user who primarily suffered as a consequence.

The Labour Party's policy to replace the discredited Motorway Box scheme was to promote public transport. In 1973 their policy for Greater London Transport was announced to include a 'low flat fare scheme leading to a free transport system which is our long term aim.' Fares were kept stable for a few years and the fare relief grant was raised to over 30 per cent of expenditure. Transport was not a particularly strong issue in the 1977 GLC election which was largely overshadowed by national politics and the performance of the minority Labour government in their pact with the Liberals. The Conservatives regained power in London and in May 1977 published their policy for London Transport, *London Transport – A New Look*, which placed much greater emphasis on financial viability than transport planning. Fare relief was cut to 18 per cent and the fare increases that followed brought London to the brink of a public transport strike in June 1979.

In the London Transport Executive's Annual Report for 1979, Ralph Bennett, the chairman, asserted that it had 'proved difficult to establish long-term policies and objectives for the future of public transport in London because of changes in political control and priorities'. In 1981 Labour was returned to power in London, with transport policy featuring prominently in their election campaign. Labour had pledged to reduce public transport fares, had won the election and proceeded to implement the largest public transport development scheme the capital had seen. Entitled 'Fares Fair', the plan involved the introduction of a totally new zonal fares system, the use of 'Travelcards' to replace season tickets and the general reduction in fares by 25 per cent. Fares Fair came into effect in October 1981 and its effects were both rapid and greater than had been expected. Passenger mileage and revenue went up substantially, car usage and congestion dropped, and in consequence so did road accidents.

But the 'Left/Right' battle over public transport was not to wait until the next GLC election. The Conservative-controlled London Borough of Bromley took the GLC to court, claiming that the supplementary rate levied to finance the new transport policy was illegal. The High Court dismissed the case, the judge commenting that transport policy was not an area in which the judiciary should become involved. But Bromley appealed against the ruling. To the astonishment of the GLC (and the delight of the Conservative government), a panel of Court of Appeal judges chaired by Lord Denning ruled that the subsidies were illegal due to the wording of the 1969 Act under which the GLC had taken over London Transport. Indeed the ruling went so far as to suggest that any subsidy for London Transport was illegal. The Denning ruling was upheld in the House of Lords. Labour's election pledge had been overturned by the judiciary.

Fares Fair had been in force for only two months. The GLC was now unable to pay London Transport the subsidy to compensate for reducing fares. As a consequence London Transport was heading for a loss in excess of £60 million. The only legal way out was to double fares and cut bus and tube services, which was what happened in March 1982.

The end result was that London Transport was in a worse mess than ever. Bus services were particularly badly affected by the fare rises and traffic levels on London's roads rose sharply. A study of the number of road accidents following the fare rise was conducted by the Transport Studies Group of University College London. This concluded that in one year alone, Lord Denning's ruling ending Fares Fair had led to 50 extra deaths, 600 more serious injuries and a further 5,750 minor injuries.

Following legal advice, the GLC introduced a new fares reduction scheme in April 1983 which could not be challenged in the courts. This involved the extension of the 'Travelcard' system, a merger of some of the fare zones and a modest reduction in fares. The results of this again exceeded expectations with £25 million more revenue being generated than was expected. In their London Transport Plan, the GLC envisaged fares remaining stable in cash terms with the subsidy to London Transport at around £220 million a year. This it was envisaged would raise passenger mileage from 4,805 million in 1983 to 5,770 million by 1987. Accidents would drop and the reduced traffic levels would reduce congestion, making London Transport's bus operations more economical and reducing road repair and construction bills.

But there was to be no period of stability in transport policy for London. All the Metropolitan Counties, as well as Greater London, were controlled by Labour administrations and all had introduced public transport promotion policies involving fares reductions. This did not please the Conservative government in Westminster, intent on reducing public expenditure, with the two major exceptions of defence and roads. Their solution was simple and frightening. If they were unable to win control of these councils by the ballot box, they would simply abolish them. As an official legal entity, London would cease to exist together with the six Metropolitan Counties. They would all become just a group of adjoining Boroughs.

At the time this book went to press the outcome of the political wrangle over the abolition of the GLC and Metropolitan Counties had yet to be resolved. The 'paving' bill to abolish the 1985 elections to these authorities was resoundingly defeated in the House of Lords, but plans to abolish the Metropolitan Counties and the GLC were still proceeding.

As a forerunner, the 1984 Transport Act removed London Transport from the GLC and, from 29 June 1984, vested it in the government-run London Regional Transport Authority. Although the LRTA is required 'to have due regard to the transport needs for the time being of Greater London', this is only within the financial objectives set by the Minister for Transport. The subsidy for London Regional Transport (the new name for London Transport) is being cut to £95 million and, although the stated policy is that fares will only increase in line with inflation, in practice it looks as though this level of subsidy will require much steeper rises. The first fares increase took effect from January 1985. How many will die as a result of this in increased road accidents has yet to be seen.

Road policies for the moment remain with the GLC, but are expected to be passed to a joint government/London Borough 'quango'. A £4,000 million plan to develop London's roads in total isolation from other transport and planning considerations is mooted. This would be the largest roads scheme since the discredited Motorway Box was abandoned in 1973.

The administrative framework for transport planning has been totally dismantled and scattered among a variety of central, local and pseudo-government authorities. No overall co-ordinating transport authority exists now for London, and before long the same will be true for all of Britain's major cities. The battle between 'left' and 'right' continues and escalates. Its cost has never been estimated.

Paris's political consensus

The way in which transport policy has been affected by the 'left'/'right' political swings in Britain is out of step with the experience of other European cities. Though the 'left'/'right' division can be equally as sharp, and the building of urban motorways just as controversial, public transport has not emerged as the politically divisive issue it is here in Britain. Plans to develop the public transport networks of European cities have enjoyed a considerable amount of political consensus and hence have made substantially better progress than in the UK.

In Paris, for instance, the promoters of urban motorway building were from the 'right' of the political spectrum, but so too were the champions of publicly funded public transport. The triumph of the plan for investment in public transport in preference to motorway construction in Paris may have come after fierce battles, but they did not polarise the 'left' and the 'right' as has been the tendency in Britain. There was certainly nothing like the way in which the Labour GLC's pro-public transport policies have resulted in London Transport being taken away from them by an anti-public transport Conservative government.

Public ownership of transport has a longer history in France than in Britain. There has always been a tradition of state initiative leading the private sector and state ownership tends to be viewed more as complementary to the private sector than a threat, as is portrayed in Britain. In France, public transport, rather than being nationalised in one go, was taken into public ownership piecemeal, beginning in 1878 and completed by 1938. Public transport in Paris was reorganised in 1948 when RATP (Régie Autonome des Transports Publiques) was set up.

The development of Paris up to the 1950s was totally different from London's mushrooming growth and decentralising population and industry. There was extraordinarily little development from the time the Metro was built until the mid-1950s. Paris suffered little war damage and the population remained unchanged at around 2.9 million. Industry remained sited centrally: the Citroen factory, just beyond the Eiffel Tower, was in no way unusual.

Paris in the 1950s was, by the standards of the world, a backward city. But then for two decades it grew faster than any city in the industrialised world, save for those in Japan. Road facilities were very quickly developed. Between the mid-1950s and early 1970s, the Périphérique was constructed – a motorway encircling the whole central area – and an inner-city motorway was built along the right bank of the Seine. The beautiful boulevards, built by Haussmann, became mostly one-way, and outside Paris toll-motorways linked the city in all directions with its region and beyond.

As in Britain in the late 1950s and early 60s, public transport was out of fashion with government and planners. All their interest was devoted to the car and traffic, and public transport stagnated. The turnaround came in 1965, when a plan for the Paris region was published. This plan, *Schème Directeur d'Amenagement et d'Urbanisme de la Region Parisienne*, suggested some ways by which the Paris conurbation could build up to a population of 15 million by the year 2000.

This reinforced government thinking, developed a few years earlier, about renewing the centre of Paris on a gigantic scale. Under President Pompidou a plan was devised which even put Buchanan's schemes in *Traffic in Towns* into the shade for its sheer cost and destruction. In this plan, suburban centres were to be developed together with eight suburban 'new towns' along the valley of the Seine. Although the term 'new town' was used, they were effectively an urban extension of Paris, not towns in their own right. For the old city a complete transformation was envisaged. Much of the existing housing was to be ripped down to make room for an elaborate motorway network and in its place great tower blocks were to rise providing space for new offices and luxury flats. The existing inhabitants were not

LEGEND

◼ URBAN CENTER

☐ PREFECTURE

▥ ZONE OF NEW URBANIZATION

▥ ZONE OF NEW URBANIZATION (EXACT LOCATIONS NOT YET DETERMINED)

▥ CURRENT URBANIZED AREA

▢ OPEN SPACE, FORESTS, AND LARGE RECREATIONAL AREAS

═ MAJOR ROADS

┿-- RAILROAD LINES EXISTING AND PLANNED

8
The 1965 master plan for the Paris region. This envisaged the expansion of Paris by the construction of eight suburban 'new towns' (two were subsequently dropped), massive urban motorway network and four new regional railway lines (the Reseau Express Regional).

catered for in the centre, but would have to move to the periphery. President Pompidou stated quite plainly: 'Paris must be adapted to the automobile.'

Opposition to this plan was intense, but it was only with the death of President Pompidou that a change in policy occurred. The plans for the expansion of Paris and the construction of the suburban 'new towns' continued, but under President Giscard d'Estaing, elected in 1974, the 'motorways and tower blocks' vision of central Paris was totally scrapped. Giscard d'Estaing personally ordered that no more tower blocks should be constructed and that all large-scale development in inner Paris should be abandoned. The plan to build a motorway along the left bank of the Seine was dropped. Jacques Chirac, soon to be Mayor of Paris, denounced the decision not to build the left bank motorway as 'a piece of demagogy'. The project, he said, 'was inevitably inscribed in the geography of Paris and dropping it is a major error, one of the great errors of our time.'

115

But the advocates of motorways and tower blocks had lost. Their time had passed. From 1976 restrictions on the use of cars intensified and investment and expansion of the Metro was increased. The automobile was being adapted to Paris.

Developing the Metro

The pricing of public transport was an issue in Paris as it has been in London, although the need for some public subsidy was recognised earlier. In the 1950s and 1960s, the level of subsidy was as low as in London and the same pattern of rising fares and falling passengers was experienced. For example, in 1952 Paris buses were carrying more than 470,000 passengers daily, but the cost of short trips soared following the introduction of a common ticket for bus and Metro. Sixty per cent of the passengers drifted away. Up until the mid-1970s fares continued to rise in real terms, though the French were quicker and more vociferous at their protests over high fares than London Transport customers.

But with the turnaround in transport policy in 1976, there came the introduction of a monthly card for use on bus and Metro without restriction. It cost around £8.50 for the month with higher priced cards for use in the outer suburbs and on suburban bus services. The zonal Carte Orange system reduced most commuters' travel costs by about 50 per cent, undercutting the cost of bringing a car into the city.

The fares policy was complemented with considerable investment in the Metro and in the Reseau Express Regional (RER). The latter is a sort of 'super' Metro – a regional commuter railway that dated back to the Gaullist era. It was the popular legacy of General de Gaulle's grandiose schemes like the La Defence skyscraper, tower blocks, the liner *France* and the French half of Concorde. Its development had fitted in with Pompidou's plans to extend Paris by the construction of the new towns, but in practice it has come to serve a considerably more positive role under modern transport planning in France.

More than any other scheme, the RER, some 55 miles of new suburban metro-style railway serving a population of 10 million, created a new lifestyle for Paris and its hinterland. The extremes of the line to Saint-Germain-en-Laye in the west to Boissy-Saint-Leger in the east had been approaching each other since 1969. On 9 December 1977 the largest Metro station in the world opened at Châtelet-les-Halles. The RER was complete, ending both the insularity of the city of Paris and the isolation of the rural areas of the Ile de France. Half a million people had moved from the city to live in the dormitory new towns and new suburban areas near the RER, while millions more were drawn into the commuter network from areas that were previously viewed as provincial backwaters.

London's never ending transport problems – when will transport planning be taken seriously?
(Photo: Stephen Potter)

Lessons for London?

Today about 65 per cent of the revenue for Paris's public transport services comes from state subsidies, coupled with a vigorous policy of investment in the Metro and buses. Should this be a model for London, or is Paris's experience unique? A number of transport researchers have attempted to answer this question, but it is doubtful whether this is a question of relevance to our transport policy crisis. The main reason why London's public transport services have lurched from crisis to crisis, with only brief periods of consolidation in between, has nothing to do with the transport planning techniques used. It is simply that transport planning does not exist in this country. If it did, then the inconsistencies and inefficiencies of the London Transport tragedy would have been ironed out. Instead we are further away than we ever were from getting a decent transport system for London.

Transport policy is a mere byproduct of other political objectives as the parties battle their ideologies out over the buses, trains and tubes. Until this is ended and coherent transport planning is developed, Britain's transport system is destined to be the poor relation of almost any other comparable country. The reason why public transport in Paris is so good is that both the 'right' and the 'left' in France take transport planning seriously.

9 Limited change

The focus changes

In the decade from the mid-1950s to the mid-1960s the overwhelming preoccupation in transport planning and research was how modern society could accommodate mass car ownership and use. Difficult though this problem was, the focus of attention gradually switched to the consequences created by mass car use. Though it may not be easy or popular to destroy the centres of all major towns and cities in order that all who have a car may use it, and rebuild them in the same style as Los Angeles or Milton Keynes, this is not the greater challenge. The real problem is that, even under relatively low levels of car ownership, the effect of the car as a transport system upon all other methods of travel is pretty devastating.

This was touched upon in Chapter 7, particularly with reference to the alternative design of new towns where it was shown that a 'full motorisation' urban structure makes travel by foot, cycle and public transport difficult or impossible. This is because the sort of city structure most suited to the car is that least suited to all other methods of travel.

But new towns are built by planners. Surely the same cannot be said of existing cities? But it can. Entirely normal, unplanned market mechanisms are gradually, but relentlessly, transforming our urban and rural environments into a Buchanan-like full motorisation structure. The car user, predominantly the better-off in society, is encouraging the development of low-density, sprawling suburbs or semi-urbanised metropolitan villages. Such areas are difficult for public transport to serve at all, let alone provide an adequate service. Equally the car user has encouraged the development of large, out-of-town shopping centres and hypermarkets to the detriment of existing town centre and neighbourhood facilities. Not only does this hit public transport, but by having shops and all facilities spread more widely, motorised travel has become necessary for more and more journey purposes. The range of facilities available to pedestrians has shrunk significantly.

But it was not only the social effects of car ownership that led to new transport policies being considered from the second half of the 1960s; the whole vision of a prosperous and leisured future was beginning to crumble. Up until then, the only conceivable vision of Britain in the 1990s and beyond was of a society where all major problems were of affluence and leisure. The 1967 Six Day War in the Middle East was the first event really to shake this vision, with the realisation of how vulnerable the West's prosperity and economic growth really was. As the concern for one rigid view of the future melted with Britain's slide into the recession of the late 1970s and 80s, so the focus of transport policy and research shifted away from unattainable dreams to present realities.

But the forces that had brought about the dream continued to have a real and persistent impact upon reality. The effect that growing car use had on the profitability of public transport operations meant that by the mid-1960s there were few private operators at all still in business. Although many of the larger municipal bus companies did provide subsidies, there was no proper mechanism for regular state support. Car ownership had not as yet extended to half of Britain's households, and transport studies were beginning to show that, even under unduly optimistic economic conditions, 'universal' car ownership would never occur. There would always be a hard core of 15 to 20 per cent of households who would not wish, or have the resources, to own a car. Added to this, studies of households with cars indicated that access to the household car was often remarkably limited.

Transport realities

An important and influential study of personal travel patterns was *Personal Mobility and Transport Policy* (1973) by Mayer Hillman, Irwin Henderson and Anne Whalley. This examined personal mobility (the ability of individuals to travel) in five contrasting areas: a small parish in Oxfordshire, a ward of a 30,000 population town, a neighbourhood in a 60,000 population new town, a medium size suburb on the outskirts of a 300,000 population city, and an inner London borough.

This survey showed that access to cars, even in car-owning households, was severely limited to certain types of people. The contrast between men and women was of particular note (Table 4).

Table 4   Level of access to car by sex of adults and area (%)

Level	Rurage Man	Rurage Woman	Smallish Man	Smallish Woman	Newton Man	Newton Woman	Suburbury Man	Suburbury Woman	Lonborough Man	Lonborough Woman
1	67	33	70	36	64	14	54	8	40	13
2	6	31	7	27	3	45	1	30	7	25
3	8	2	7	3	10	5	10	2	9	1
4	20	34	16	34	24	37	35	60	44	61
	100	100	100	100	100	100	100	100	100	100

Level 1 = Car licence holder in a car-owning household
Level 2 = Non-licence holder in a car-owning household
Level 3 = Licence holder in a non-car-owning household
Level 4 = Non-licence holder in a non-car-owning household
Source: Hillman *et al.*, 1973, p. 55.

This research showed that the use of a car, even in a car-owning household, tends to be very selective. Cars are predominantly used by adult men and the travel needs of other household members fitted around their wishes. More recent information from the National Travel Survey supports such a view (Table 5).

Table 5   Travel methods according to age/sex of person

	Per cent of all journeys by					Journeys (000s)
	Walk/ Cycle	Car driver	Car passenger	Public transport	Other	
Child under 10	57	0	35	8	1	65
Teenagers, 11–20	53	6	18	20	3	83
Men aged 21–64	25	57	7	9	2	144
Women aged 21–59	42	21	23	14	1	122
Men 65 and over	52	25	6	16	1	100
Women 60 and over	50	6	19	25	1	100

Source: 1978–9 National Travel Survey from Potter, 1982.

The overwhelming conclusion of Hillman's study was that there are very contrasting travel patterns between different groups in society. People had differing levels of access to different types of transport, particularly the car. Transport policy just did not seem to reflect this. It had one preoccupation – the car driver. Hillman concluded that

> personal mobility has not been treated as the object of policy. Indeed a piecemeal approach has grown up over the years, removed from the reality of people's lives: preoccupations with traffic flows, be they pedestrian or vehicular, with the long-term as opposed to the immediate, and with a 'scientific' approach as opposed to one attempting to solve problems. All these have caused an imbalance between the worlds of reality and policy. . . . Few attempts have been made to face up to the deep conflicts that exist between the differing requirements of people using different methods of travel. Transport policies can no longer be assumed to have only narrow social and environmental implications and cannot ignore effects on personal mobility.

The idea that Buchananite traffic planning was the way forward for society as a whole had crumbled. It clearly advantaged certain sectors of society to the cost of others. Transport policy had just grown out of the mix of interests of the road industry, planners, the railways and (to some extent) the bus industry. The end result was in no way actually related to people's travel needs. That did not seem to be relevant to 'transport' policy as it had evolved in Britain.

The 1968 Transport Act

The 1968 Transport Act was the first recognition by government that people's travel needs were an important consideration in transport policy. It pre-dated Hillman's study, and was mainly designed to ensure that public transport services were not eroded by rising car ownership and use. It was nevertheless a response that in no way challenged the powerful forces of the 'road lobby', but endeavoured to tidy up the nastier consequences of their actions. This total isolation from the cause of transport problems may well be viewed as a fundamental weakness of the 1968 Act, but the road lobby at this time was very strong. This was the era of London's Motorway Box plan and the draft plan for Milton Keynes had just been published. The Transport Minister of the time, Barbara Castle, very much recognised the political limitations of her post:

> When I took over as Minister of Transport (1965) the most vociferous lobby in this country was that represented by road interests. The propaganda and pressure groups led by the British Road Federation said that we must concentrate all our resources on building the first 1,000 miles of motorway. The environment lobby had barely been born, and when I tried to suggest that there were other considerations that we should bear in mind I had an uphill task because about the whole of public opinion and the then opposition were against me. (Barbara Castle, quoted in Hamer, 1974, p. 1)

The 1968 Transport Act therefore sought to reorganise the provision of public transport and to arrange government subsidies on a regular basis in order that a reasonable service could be maintained in the face of the failing operational environment. This very much set the criteria for state intervention in public transport as 'social need'. The concept of intervention for transport planning purposes (of which social need is but a part) was not politically on.

The basic concept of the 1968 Transport Act was to provide large, efficiently run operating units for public transport, which it was hoped could benefit from economies of scale. In the provincial conurbations Passenger Transport Executives were established, very similar in concept to the London Transport Executive which continued in being. These took over the municipal and other state-owned bus services in their areas. Policy for the Passenger Transport Executives was decided by Passenger Transport Authorities, who were directly appointed by the Minister of Transport to oversee their Executives. Four PTEs were initially established: Merseyside, Greater Manchester, West Midlands and Tyneside. In 1973, after the reform of local government, a fifth was established for Greater Glasgow.

Outside of London and the metropolitan conurbations, the National Bus Company (NBC) and Scottish Bus Group were formed to run the remaining nationalised bus sector through large regional subsidiaries. They also ran services acquired voluntarily from private operators. With declining

70
Bus lane in Edinburgh's Princes Street.
Edinburgh has a municipal bus service and the city authority has in recent years developed a number of bus priority schemes. (Photo: Stephen Potter)

profitability, the private sector had shrunk rapidly, and in 1968 the two largest remaining private companies were voluntarily acquired by NBC. About fifty municipal bus companies continued, mainly to be found in the larger towns and cities outside the conurbations.

Given this reorganisation of bus services, the 1968 Transport Act also introduced capital and revenue grants for public transport operations. Although the PTEs did not take over British Rail services in their areas, the PTAs were given access to specific grants to subsidise 'socially necessary' rail services and ended up being responsible for most commuter lines in their areas.

The original structure of the 1968 Act only lasted for six years when the reform of local government under the 1972 Local Government Act imposed further reorganisational changes. This particularly affected the PTE/PTA areas, for larger local authorities were established in the conurbations. The five PTAs were taken over by the new Metropolitan Councils and two new Passenger Transport Executives were created for the metropolitan counties of West and South Yorkshire. In Scotland, Strathclyde Regional Council took over the Glasgow PTE and in London the GLC had already (in 1969) taken over the London Transport Executive under separate legislation.

This move was significant and went a long way towards making possible what Hillman had been calling for. Transport planning functions were now combined in the same state authority. The Metropolitan Counties were responsible for both running public transport and highway planning. There existed a co-ordinating authority which would have to find ways to decide how to allocate resources to these areas. Integrated transport planning, previously only really possible in the uniquely planned new towns, was on the cards for Britain's major cities. Furthermore, although the other county authorities did not run their public transport services, they were given direct transport planning responsibilities, including roads, subsidising public transport and providing for pedestrians and cyclists.

From 1975–6, County and Metropolitan Councils submitted annual Transport Policy and Programmes (TPP) for their areas to the Department of the Environment (into which the Ministry of Transport had been merged, although it was soon separated again). These specified the transport planning objectives for the county, current expenditure proposals, priorities and progress *for all methods of travel*. The Department of the Environment would then assess the contents of the TPP and approve a total level of expenditure, paid in terms of a rate support grant and a transport supplementary grant to build roads, car parks, railways, footpaths and cycleways or to subsidise buses and trains. The 1978 Transport Act reinforced the counties' role by making it a duty for each shire county to prepare five-year passenger transport plans.

For sixty years, county authorities had built roads on the basis of bids to central government for funds. Around this function had built up a whole urban planning and design philosophy. From the mid-1970s the same applied to all travel methods. So did this now mean that integrated transport planning had at last become a reality in Britain?

71
San Diego Bike Bus. All buses in San Diego, California, have bike racks fitted on the back. It is a very cheap and simple method of transport integration. Given the political and administrative will, transport integration can yield enormous benefits.
(Photo: Stephen Potter)

At a national level, the answer is undoubtably no. For although the legislation permitted integrated transport planning to occur, it also permitted virtually anything else, including the continuation of divisive 'full motorisation' plans. However, particularly among the new metropolitan counties, real transport planning did begin to emerge.

The Tyne and Wear Metro

Probably the most extensive use of the transport planning powers vested in the PTEs and the metropolitan councils is that of the Tyne and Wear Metro. This was conceived in 1971 when the former Tyneside Passenger Transport Authority and Executive made recommendations for the area stemming from the Tyne and Wear Plan. At this time the area was run by a number of separate local authorities who had the foresight to commission a joint planning report for the whole Tyneside area.

The Tyne and Wear Plan identified major weaknesses in the public transport services of the area. In particular it pointed out that:

1 Existing public transport services were not properly integrated.
2 Bus services were suffering badly from road congestion.
3 The road-building programme in Tyne and Wear, although extensive, was not addressing the problems of mobility in this area and further roads would involve considerable destruction.
4 The existing rail network failed to serve the city centre of Newcastle.
5 The existing rail services had become run-down, and were operated by elderly and slow diesels which made a loss of £1.5 million per annum.

The study plan considered a number of alternatives ranging from more road investment and an enhanced bus service through to a massively improved suburban rail system. These showed that the rail network offered considerable potential as the basis of a light rail Metro system, similar to the 'super-trams' being introduced on the Continent. This, integrated in with bus routes, British Rail's local services and ferries, was viewed as the better alternative to fulfilling the transport needs of the people of Tyneside than the motorway option.

It must be emphasised that the Tyne and Wear Metro concept is not just the building of an urban light railway. The more important element is the careful and effective planning of all transport services to ensure that all sectors of society have the means and ability to travel and that public resources are not wasted on transport investments that only aid one group of people to the detriment of another. It was the first truly comprehensive approach to transport provision in any major British city. This produced clearly defined transport planning objectives which in turn led to the idea

73
Gateshead Transport Interchange. Bus and Metro services are carefully integrated, with the bus station being positioned directly above the Metro station and timetables carefully designed to connect the services. (Photo: Tyne and Wear Passenger Transport Executive)

72
The Tyne and Wear Metro. A Metro Car entering Gateshead station. The 84-seat cars can be operated singly, or coupled together in pairs. This is part of the new underground section of the Metro where a three-minute peak hour frequency is provided. The electrification system used is 1,500v overhead lines.
(Photo: Tyne and Wear Passenger Transport Executive)

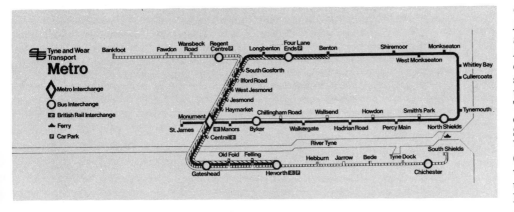

74
Diagrammatic Map of the Tyne and Wear Metro. The Metro currently has forty-one stations, with two more under construction. There are plans to extend the lines to Sunderland, via Washington New Town (whose station and line was closed in 1964 under the Beeching Plan) and to Newcastle Airport, Killingworth and Whiteleas.
(Map: Tyne and Wear Passenger Transport Executive)

for the 'super-tram' Metro lines, together with their linking bus, rail and ferry services and the 'transport interchanges' with their car parks and easy changing between different types of transport. As in the new town plans, once comprehensive transport planning was used, full motorisation options were found to be frighteningly expensive in terms of public expenditure and were utterly incapable of achieving the transport planning goals set.

The key to the Metro plan was for Tyne and Wear to take over the existing British Rail track, electrify and upgrade it, and to construct new underground links through the centre of Newcastle so as to join the north and south Tyneside railways. A joint working party from the PTE and British Rail developed the idea which became the basis of the Tyneside Metropolitan Railway Bill which received the Royal Assent in July 1973. The first section of the Metro was opened in 1980 and the complete network was operational by 1984. The system is now being developed further, with new stations under construction and plans to extend the Metro to Washington New Town and to Newcastle Airport.

The scale and speed of construction of the Tyne and Wear Metro stands in strong contrast to the piecemeal and stop/go policies of other urban transport authorities. In ten years a city-wide mass transit system of 34 miles of track (4 miles of which is new underground line), consisting of four Metrolines serving 41 stations – moved from being a plan to reality. No other city authority in the world has planned and built so large a Metro so quickly. The people of Tyne and Wear are rightly proud of their Metro.

Bus services were revised to fit into the Metro, acting as 'feeders' as well as serving areas to which the Metro did not extend. Through ticketing was an important element of the integration of Tyne and Wear's transport plan as was the provision of extensive 'park and ride' facilities at key suburban stations. Low fares form part of the system, in order to attract car users on to public transport and ensure that congestion and accidents are reduced as well as to remove the need for expensive road construction. However, the emphasis is very much on capital investment and planning to achieve an attractive public transport system rather than price.

The Tyne and Wear Metro has been a remarkable success story in integrated transport planning. This relatively low-cost method of developing a light rail network has led to similar schemes being proposed for Bristol and Manchester. In London, a Metro-type light railway is now under construction linking new developments in Docklands along disused railway lines and some new track to the City of London. This has effectively replaced an extension of the Jubilee tube line.

Public transport investment or low fares?

In some cities and conurbations, the construction of an extensive Metro system is less easy than in Tyne and Wear. The South Yorkshire conurbation, centred on Sheffield, is an example. Here resources, instead of being concentrated on capital investments, have been predominantly used to provide revenue subsidies to bus fares. Indeed this could be viewed as representing an alternative approach to Tyne and Wear's high-investment option. The level of revenue subsidy received by public transport in British cities is amongst the lowest in the developed world. In 1979, 25 per cent of London Transport's operating costs were met from subsidies compared to Brussels at 70 per cent, West Berlin 61 per cent, Paris 56 per cent, Milan 71 per cent and New York at 72 per cent. The only area in Britain to have a subsidy level approaching that found abroad is South Yorkshire at 65 per cent (Allen, 1981). There have been no fare rises in South Yorkshire now for ten years, and as such in real terms (allowing for inflation) bus and rail fares within South Yorkshire have dropped to well below the cost of travelling by car. It is even cheaper to go by bus than to have four or five people crammed into a Mini!

As in Tyne and Wear, this support to public transport stems from an integrated approach to transport planning. Patronage on local bus and rail services has increased dramatically and new and better buses and trains have been introduced to cope with the demand.

The main disadvantage of the South Yorkshire option is that it depends almost entirely upon price to succeed. Bus services have been improved and a number of investments taken place, but nothing of the sort of improvement in the *quality* of public transport that has occurred at Tyne and Wear or in other cities (like Liverpool and Glasgow) where the rail network has been improved.

Motorists often underestimate the costs of travelling by car and many (about 1.5 million) receive company subsidies, a large amount of which effectively comes from the state via tax concessions. In addition, buses do not have the same image of reliability and acceptability that an underground or rail service enjoys. Travelling by train or tube is socially acceptable. Bus travel has a less attractive image among many car drivers. As such, for price alone to be an effective tool of transport planning requires bus fares to be reduced to almost negligible levels, as in South Yorkshire, to have much of an impact on road traffic.

A second disadvantage of a 'low fares only' policy is that it can be so easily reversed. As was discussed in Chapter 8, this has been the experience of London and, with the proposed abolition of the Metropolitan Counties, could well occur in South Yorkshire also. Whatever happens to fares in Tyne and Wear, the increased quality of service that the building of the Metro has produced will remain.

The answer to this problem, and that adopted by many European countries and in the USA, is to go both for high investment *and* low fares. This has been the case in Paris and in the many American cities where extensive new Metros have been built over the past twenty years. The experience of the USA is particularly of note, where the cost of new Metros is written off in government grants, *and* fare subsidies totalling 50 per cent or more of operational costs are provided. In Britain, capital costs are not written off in this way but are treated as loans, and fare subsidies rarely exceed 10 per cent.

The questions as to the most effective methods of applying integrated transport planning, the mix of revenue support and capital investment and the goals to be set, have now been overtaken by a threat to the whole concept and structure of integrated transport planning itself. The entire integrating structure of the 1968 Transport Act and the 1972 Local Government Act is due to be dismantled with the abolition of the GLC and the Metropolitan Counties. Transport responsibilities are to be scattered between district and borough authorities, central government and a host of appointed executives and joint authority committees. In addition, current government plans for bus route deregulation will make even rudimentary planning for public transport difficult and integrated transport planning virtually impossible. The reasons for this bear no relationship to transport planning and the practical outcome portrays a very uncertain future for public transport in our cities.

Integrated transport planning is possible and it works. We can reduce the mobility gap and provide access for all. That is if our councils and government wish to.

10 Losing track?

What overall impression is there of the way in which transport developments have affected the society, economy and life of modern Britain? Has it been a rational and popular process reflecting the true desires of people and the democratic nature of Great Britain, or simply the outcome of a tussle between powerful vested interests, in which the needs of the general public were manipulated rather than being served? It seems clear that elements of both arguments ring true from the evidence that this book contains.

What of the future for transport policy? Transport planning has been developed in Britain and has succeeded in the places that have had the courage to implement it fully. Is the current dismantling of the administration for transport planning a temporary setback, or have we seen the end of all attempts to reconcile the conflicting demands of private transport, public transport and the pedestrian?

One crucial idea is that no one form of transport can adequately cater for all people at all times. A mix of the basic travel methods of walking, cycling, public and private transport is needed. We need a transport system which provides adequately for all four and ensures that each can provide a high quality of service without adversely affecting another. The way in which car use, in particular, erodes the quality of travel for non-car users is a crucial lesson, not just for Britain, but of international importance.

From the individual's viewpoint, what is the experience of the changes in these different transport modes over the last thirty or so years?

For the car user, travel has become safer, faster and simpler with the coming of the motorways and the vast national investment in upgrading the nation's road network. Despite moans about the price of petrol, the cost of car ownership has, in reality, declined. This was particularly so up to the early 1970s, after which car and petrol prices rose in real terms for a while before settling down. Once more the real trend in petrol prices is down.

Whether this will continue to be so in the long term is another matter, should electric vehicles become necessary. The economics of electrically powered vehicles are very different to that of the internal combustion engine. Running costs are lower but capital costs are much higher. This is largely because a battery pack, costing £2,000 or more and needing to be replaced every three or four years, will replace the petrol tank, costing £20 and lasting the lifetime of a car. Whatever advances in battery technology may occur, they will never overcome this price difference, which is why electric cars have never caught on.

It is to be expected then that in the long term the costs of car ownership

75
*A new section of the A5
in Buckinghamshire.
New roads make car
travel a lot easier than
twenty years ago.
(Photo: Stephen Potter)*

will rise considerably, but for the moment cars are relatively cheap. How exactly we will adjust to this transition is a matter for speculation, but there are indications that road interests will step in to stop car ownership falling. The reason for believing this is that it has already happened.

During the recession of the late 1970s and 1980s there has been no let-up in the demand for cars, and traffic levels have continued to rise. With well over 3 million unemployed, with many more on short time or reduced wages, this seems a perplexing paradox. But the truth of the matter is that car ownership and use is now subsidised far more heavily than public transport. Since the mid-1970s, company purchases of cars have increased substantially to the extent that they now consist of over half the new car market. The reason for this growth is largely linked to the way in which company cars are taxed. The methods used result in both the individual

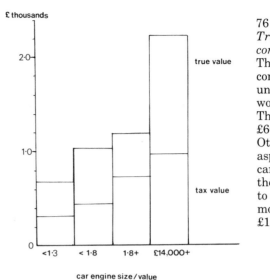

£ thousands

car engine size / value

76
True and tax value of company-provided cars. The state subsidises company cars by undervaluing their worth for tax purposes. This subsidy is about £600m per annum. Other tax avoidance aspects of income as cars and motoring takes the total state subsidy to company-assisted motoring to around £1,500m a year.

Table 6   *Household vehicle ownership* in Britain*

Vehicle ownership or use of	% of households
Three or more cars	1
Two cars	10
One car	46
Motor cycles only	2
Bicycles only	8
No vehicles	33
Total	100 (8,007 households in sample)

*Figures relate to vehicles *available* to a household to allow for company cars and cars hired or on loan.
Source: 1978–9 National Travel Survey from Potter, 1982.

car user and the company paying substantially less tax than if the individual had the equivalent sum in cash (see TEST Report *The Company Car Factor*, 1985). The tax loss represents an effective government subsidy to private motoring of at least £1.5 billion per annum.

With the companies and the government providing the initial outlay for half the cars passing on to the second-hand market, the cost to individuals has been significantly reduced. Indeed it is probably this factor that has maintained the growth in car ownership through the late 1970s and into the recession of the 1980s. Private car purchases peaked in around 1972 and have declined ever since. The original tax loophole may not have been the product of road lobby pressure, but road interests have certainly thwarted even powerful Treasury attempts to close it. The state subsidy to motoring remains and, unlike that to public transport, has enjoyed an unquestioned expansion.

Table 7   *Methods of travel in different types of area in Britain*

| Type of settlement | Public transport | Percentage of journeys by | | |
		Car	Walk	Other†
London	17	41	37	4
Birmingham	18	37	42	4
Manchester	17	35	44	4
Glasgow	26	22	49	3
Liverpool	24	30	43	4
Areas of population:				
250,000 1 million	17	40	40	5
100 ‹ 250,000	14	43	38	6
50 ‹ 100,000	13	42	39	6
25 ‹ 50,000	9	43	41	7
3 ‹ 25,000	8	44	42	5
Under 3,000	7	55	30	8
Total	12	43	39	5

†'Other' is largely bicycle, but includes motorcycle, air and water.
Source: 1978–9 National Travel Survey, from Potter, 1982.

Today about 60 per cent of the households in Britain own a car, or have the use of a company car. Travel by car accounts for 43 per cent of all journeys made (Tables 6 and 7).

What is probably surprising to many people looking at these survey figures is that, as Hillman pointed out a decade ago in *Personal Mobility and Transport Policy*, car travel falls well short of half of the journeys made in Britain and yet the car has clearly had an enormous impact on our society and economy. Car travel is extremely convenient and only moderately expensive, so it is not surprising that it is now very popular. Nevertheless, it is by no means a universal travel method.

The consequences of mass car ownership

The impact of mass car ownership has clearly produced its problems, in terms of environment, economic and transport effects. The environmental effects, despite being the easiest to address, have never been satisfactorily tackled. The trouble is that the only way that powerful economic and motoring interests will allow these to be approached is as part of a programme that would make the car the only feasible form of transport for the future. Anything that errs from such a concept by, for example, seeking to aid public transport, reduce travel needs or plan transport, is immediately swept up in a mass of political controversy. A few plans have succeeded, as in Tyne and Wear and South Yorkshire and also in a couple of new towns, but generally integrated transport planning, with the needs of all sectors of society carefully considered, is not popular among the economically and politically powerful.

Hence the most common reactions are compromise and cosmetic measures to address the worse abuses of mass car use without really tackling the root causes. Road improvements, together with legislation on car maintenance standards, seat belts and drunken drivers, has kept accident levels down to around 7,000 deaths a year. But is this really 'acceptable'? It compares with an average of under 10 passenger deaths per annum on the railways. The stern opposition that faced Barbara Castle in introducing the drinking and driving legislation in the 1960s, the very late introduction of the compulsory wearing of seat belts, the often pathetic sentences handed out to those guilty of murder or manslaughter due to reckless driving, and the effective opposition to the tightening up of driving and MoT tests all indicates a remarkable complacency in our society over checking the abuses of mass car use.

Mobility has its price. If cars were banned and we were all forced to travel by trains and buses only driven by professionals then transport accidents and problems would be minimised. But such restrictions would, of course, be unacceptable. Mobility does have its price, but are we paying over the odds? Other countries have succeeded in at least modifying the power of their motor industries in such a way that the needs of the people can be balanced against narrow industrial vested interests. It can be done.

Energy and transport policy

One preoccupation of the 1970s and 80s has been energy conservation. Transport is one area where Britain's record is extremely poor. The fuel used by cars in Britain has increased by a third over the last decade. This is a lot more than would be expected. Car ownership has only gone up by a quarter and improvements in design have been such that modern cars use 15 per cent less petrol than ten years ago. Given these two trends, fuel use should only have gone up by 10 per cent at the most.

Energy conservation in road transport has a dismal record with there being little evidence of any real progress being made at all with respect to car use (Table 8). The gains in vehicle design that have yielded the 60 m.p.g. car have been totally wiped out by increased car use. The reasons for this relate through to the wider social and economic effects of the car.

First, there has been the rise of the company car. With 1.5 million of these company- and state-subsidised cars on the road, it is not surprising that their users tend to opt for the more prestigious large-engined cars and use them a lot. Were companies to buy cars similar to that of the true private market then the nation's petrol consumption would drop by at least 10 per cent (TEST, 1985). The undertaxation of company cars is slowly being addressed, but (as discussed above) its effects are hardly acknowledged in transport policy.

Table 8 *Energy consumption in Great Britain 1971–81*

Petroleum (m. tonnes)	1971	1981	% Change
Cars and motorcycles	12.13	16.09	+33
Goods vehicles	2.52	2.35	− 7
All transport	26.07	30.63	+18
Non-transport uses	38.52	22.84	−41

Total petroleum used All energy sources (m. therms)	1971	1981	% Change
Rail	597	466	−21
Road	8,897	10,722	+21
Water	454	437	− 4
Air	1,686	1,993	+18
All transport uses	11,634	13,618	+17
Non-transport uses	45,367	41,302	−10
Total energy used by final consumers	57,001	54,920	− 4

Source: Transport Statistics Great Britain, 1971–81, HMSO.

However, the wider effects of mass car ownership also have an effect on energy use. With settlements becoming more dispersed and local facilities declining, the car is creating a need for more travel, a need that only it can really adequately fulfill. People are having to travel further and to use cars more because mass car ownership encourages the wider dispersal of people and facilities. It is a self-generating cycle, but for how long can it continue? With our adequate supplies of North Sea oil, we do not seem to be too concerned that Britain is creating a society that is heavily dependent on the least energy-efficient travel methods. Quite what will happen when North Sea oil (and North Sea oil tax revenues) run out is something that, perhaps, should concern us now. The effects of transport developments on our towns and cities builds up slowly. Having adjusted to a lifestyle built around the availability of cheap cars and cheap petrol it is not possible to adjust back overnight. The transition could be quite painful.

Public transport

The face of public transport has changed significantly over the past thirty years. Long-distance services are less comprehensive, but there have been gains as well as losses. Rail services are a lot faster. In the mid 1950s an express train would travel at up to about 80 m.p.h. Today's 125 m.p.h. air-conditioned trains represent a considerable advance in both speed and

137

77
Poster in Cumbernauld town centre. True, but for how many is this possible?
(Photo: Stephen Potter)

comfort. On eleven main trunk routes out of London there were 20 per cent more trains in 1979 than in 1951 and journey times had been cut by an average of a third. Given the restricted finances under which British Rail has operated this record represents a remarkable achievement. With more fast trains being introduced and running speeds of up to 140 m.p.h. planned in the near future, further improvements seem likely.

But the railway network is smaller, and the much publicised development of deregulated coach lines (made possible by the 1980 Transport Act) tends to be in direct competition with the lucrative rail trunk routes, not the complementing of rail by developing routes poorly served by trains. The really cheap fares and luxury coaches have been introduced to compete with the trains; where there is no rail competition, such as on cross country routes, the fares are considerably higher and there are none of the luxury trimmings of in-journey videos and a drinks trolley. Free competition may have helped to force the fares down on trunk routes, but it has done nothing at all to ensure the maintenance of a comprehensive public transport network. The fierce competition is entirely concentrated on routes that would exist anyway.

78
An Intercity 125 train
(Photo: Stephen Potter)

But it is in local public transport services that the greatest changes are to be found. Generally public transport services are poorer. In many cities local suburban railway lines have shut and bus services are less frequent, the routes more sparse and the fares higher. In a few places, as has been noted in this book, real progress has been made. As such, the quality of public transport services varies immensely in towns and cities of a similar size and character. Some have excellent services and some are dire. The range of quality and price has become extreme. This is the area in which public transport has become a political football and where millions of people have suffered in consequence as 'right' and 'left' have fought their battles over the bus queues and the daily journey to work.

79
Waiting for the bus in Leeds. Is it a coincidence that all the people in these bus queues are women?

80
A Post Bus in Kent.
First introduced in
1967, there are now 176
Post Bus routes in
Britain, carrying
passengers alongside
mail in rural areas
where conventional bus
services no longer run.
But can two buses a
day be considered to
represent a public
transport service?
(Photo: The Post Office)

Rural public transport has been decimated. With the Marples/Beeching cuts in rural railways and their short-lived replacement buses, a fastly accelerating downward spiral occurred. A few attempts have been made to provide rural public transport systems that are viable at low levels of demand. The Post Bus is one example, where Post Office vans collecting mail now carry passengers too, but this only provides a somewhat indirect twice-daily service geared to post collection times. A more useful rural transport experiment has been that undertaken in East Sussex where hospital, school, WRVS, social services and stage carriage buses have been co-ordinated by a County Council 'travel broker' so as to provide an overall rural public transport service (see Potter, 1983, and Woollett, 1981). Such a positive planning approach represents the rural equivalent of urban transport planning as displayed in Tyne and Wear and under Labour's policy in the GLC. It is possible to provide a decent transport service for non-car users in rural areas, but as in the case of most urban areas, the opportunity has been ignored. Today, in most rural areas if you can't afford a car you don't live there any more if you can possibly help it.

But for both urban and rural public transport there is yet a greater threat which may well eliminate all hope of achieving improvements in public transport services. In an attempt to cut bus subsidies, the government intends to 'privatise' bus services. This of itself would not necessarily threaten the quality of public transport, but the method chosen involves the virtual demise of all public transport planning or co-ordination. The White Paper *Buses* (1984), envisages the total deregulation of bus services, with routes being open to any operator. If a private company does not provide a service then the local authority may seek tenders from bus operators to run a subsidised service. However, funds for this are to be cut substantially on the assumption that private bus operators will be able to make money on previously subsidised routes.

This structure means that public transport services cannot be planned as a whole and assumptions as to the lower level of subsidy needed are naive in the extreme. Three trial areas experimented with deregulation during 1981–4. Only one of these, Hereford, was remotely successful in reducing subsidies and fares. However, the situation there is so chaotic that even the experiment's strongest supporters denounce total deregulation as unworkable and unnecessary to achieve savings in subsidies. Fares and timetables fluctuate almost weekly, safety standards have been flouted and the police are regularly involved in disputes and fights between rival bus operators. Buses race each other to stops and have caused chaos in the city centre streets of Hereford. Concessionary fares for the elderly and children are very difficult to organise and, as competition has intensified, rural settlements have lost their bus services and off-peak services have ceased, often with little notice being given.

If total deregulation were to proceed the most likely outcome will be intense competition on profitable urban routes. This will lead to operators cutting back on marginal services, particularly in rural areas and peripheral housing estates and even off-peak services on urban routes. The need for subsidy will be greater as these services will be deprived of being part of an overall planned network, yet resources for subsidies are to be cut.

The evidence from the trial areas suggests that the large existing state bus operators will probably win in the end, as they have the competitive edge in organisation, resources and experience. But the sort of public transport network to emerge after a decade or so of deregulated chaos is a frightening vision. The carefully developed integrated urban transport systems of Tyne and Wear, Glasgow, Liverpool and Manchester are unlikely to survive. About a third of the non-London suburban railways are expected to close and even the Tyne and Wear Metro may not survive. Rural transport planning, such as East Sussex's imaginative scheme, stands no chance of survival.

The deregulation proposals are opposed by virtually the entire public transport industry, taxi operators, user groups and local authorities of all political persuasions. Even pro-privatisation Conservative councils view this as a 'muddle-headed' piece of political dogma which can only cause misery and suffering.

Walking and cycling

In a society where transport debates centre on the industrially organised transport methods of the car and public transport, the most universal and efficient methods tend to suffer by default rather than through overt conspiracies. Walking and cycling are the most universal and efficient forms of transport in existence. Walking is the most universal and the bicycle is the most energy-efficient form of transport known to humankind. The ability to walk and cycle has been eroded badly over the last thirty years, and because these travel methods have no big industries behind them and there have been no obvious crisis points, like Beeching or the Denning ruling, this degradation has attracted little attention.

Hence, although planners in the 1950s and 60s advocated the building of separate networks for cyclists and pedestrians, outside new towns very little was done. Buchanan supported the idea, but only his proposals for roads and traffic engineering achieved widespread acceptance. It is true that pedestrians have been a source of concern since the 1930s in terms of road safety, but that had nothing to do with walking as a form of transport. It was merely about how to cross roads safely. Equally many schemes for segregated footpaths treated pedestrians in the same way. The questions as to what facilities were within walking range and what could be done to improve pedestrian accessibility were never asked.

The pedestrianised town centres, totally justified in terms of making the local environment better as cars choked up previously pleasant shopping streets, were also nothing to do with walking as a form of transport. The very concept of pedestrian routes, as opposed to areas, is only finding hesitant acceptance today.

81
Stevenage cycleways and footpaths. Almost alone among the early new towns, Stevenage developed a comprehensive network of well designed cycleways and footpaths.
(Photo: Town and Country Planning Association)

82
York city centre cycle route. From the late 1970s a number of city authorities took planning for cyclists seriously. Among them was York. This is a contra-flow cycle lane up a one-way street. (Photo: Stephen Potter)

The cyclist has also suffered from such 'passive' persecution. Improved roads, grade-separated junctions, and all the aspects designed to help traffic flow are a positive hazard to a slow-moving and vulnerable vehicle like a bicycle. The recent trend in accident statistics has been for injuries to motorists to decline and injuries to cyclists and pedestrians to rise.

It was only with the rise of the 'environmental movement' and through the development of real transport planning that any attention came to be focused on walking and cycling as forms of transport. *Walking is Transport*

83
City centre cycle route, Bremen. Fitting a cycle route into city centres often calls for originality and ingenuity, as is demonstrated by this route in the north German city of Bremen. (Photo: Stephen Potter)

was the title of Mayer Hillman and Anne Whalley's 1979 study, purposely emphasising the difference in approach between treating walking as something that is only of concern in pedestrianised town centres and when cars bump into people, and treating it as the single most important way of getting around in towns and cities.

Compared to the 1950s the conditions for walking and cycling have undoubtably degenerated. Roads are busier and are less suited to cycling than they were. Walking conditions are less pleasant and even when segregated paths are provided, the design criteria seem to be more aesthetic than practical. Even the new paths built in new towns and suburban areas wind amidst trees and bushes, keeping roads and nearby houses well out of sight. They may look pretty, but on a dark night such 'muggers' paradises' positively hinder walking as a form of transport for women in particular. The male architects who design such 'attractive' paths seem not to appreciate users' needs.

On the positive side, many local authorities now recognise the need to provide specially designed routes for cyclists and in newly developed areas cycleways are becoming more common. However there is considerably resistance from traffic engineers to pander to what is, in their view, a sub-car form of life.

Transport planning and transport politics

One overwhelming disappointment must be the failure of transport planning to establish itself as a process and a profession independent of political vagaries. For although we still have a legislative structure now that permits integrated transport planning, in practice this structure is used to do anything but this in the vast majority of cases, and it seems not to be viewed as sufficiently important to be immune from the political gerrymandering we are currently witnessing.

There seem to be several underlying causes. First, although we may speak of transport/land use planning as a single process, it is in fact carried out by a variety of government and local authority departments, each of which have their own professional and political stance to defend. For example, the 'integration' of highway engineering, planning for other forms of transport and land use planning which has occurred in the last decade is often very superficial. The degree of financial and political power held by these three groups is markedly different. Highway engineering is well established and benefits from considerable industrial support and lobbying, something that is not true of planning in general. Highway engineering represents a very market-oriented approach which is carried out by the state not because of a desire for planning (in the social and economic sense of the word) but because it is an essential activity that private enterprise cannot practically fulfill. The tradition of highway engineering is more closely akin to that of the private developer than the environmental planner. It is a tradition that does not come very close to the basic ideology of planning which presumes a market failure to provide as good an environment as could be achieved if the same resources were properly co-ordinated.

Highway engineering is also predominantly a profession for men. One striking aspect about travel patterns is the differences that exist in the ways that men and women get about. Car use is dominated by men whereas the main method of travel for women is by foot. Women are far more dependent on public transport than men and have less say in the use of the family car. It seems rather a coincidence that the male-dominated profession which has the greatest influence upon transport policy decisions favours schemes that promote car use. Sexual bias can express itself in very indirect, but none the less effective ways.

The traditional highway engineering approach has been that of responding to the market demand for roadspace. Environmental planning and state intervention for other travel methods holds the contrasting philosophy of the comprehensive optimal approach, compensating for externalities, the inclusion of wider economic and social criteria, catering for the needs of all groups in society, forward planning, and all that is associated with the concept of planning.

But compared to the real political, industrial and economic power that traditional highway engineering has, it matters little that environmental planning is intellectually superior. Planning is a political weakling. The two may be technically 'co-ordinated' but in practice one carries a hundred times the influence of the other.

So you have one branch of state intervention helping to create transport problems (highway engineering) which another (planning) tries to correct but does not have the power and influence to do so. It is an inefficient, unnecessarily costly process which creates avoidable problems, inconvenience and often hardship for millions. The key to breaking out of this is not to improve planning techniques, for they are perfectly adequate, but to improve the political status of the concept of planning. The answer to the transport policy crisis has nothing to do with technical advances or the ability of 'planners'. It is purely a matter of political will and the extent to which our society is prepared to have the lives of the majority manipulated by the vested interests of a few.

There is some evidence that we are becoming aware of the dangers and problems that this has caused in transport. Transport is now no longer a low-priority, non-political subject. That was one way in which the manipulation took place. Transport policy, particularly in urban areas, has come to the fore. People are aware of the issues; they are more aware of who gains and who loses. There can be none of the 'common good' nonsense that Marples used in the early 1960s to take a hatchet to public transport and line the pockets of the road construction industry with billions of pounds of taxpayers' money. The rapid discrediting of the 1983 Serpell Report on British Rail showed this to be true.

Transport policy is now at the forefront of British politics. The resources and knowledge to develop an efficient, equitable and flexible transport system for our society exist. In the past they have been squandered and manipulated. We cannot afford to do that in the future.

References
and reading list

Adams, John (1981), *Transport Planning – Vision and Practice*, Routledge & Kegan Paul.

Allen, J. E. (1981), *Revenue Support of Public Transport*, proceedings of conference *Future of Urban Transport*, Nottingham University.

Allsop, Prof. Richard (1983), *Road Casualty Effects of London Transport Fare Changes*, Report of the Transport Studies Group, University College London to the GLC Transport Committee, No. T937.

Bagwell, Philip S. (1968), *The Railway Clearing House in the British Economy, 1842–1922*, Allen & Unwin.

Bagwell, Philip S. (1974), *The Transport Revolution from 1970*, Batsford.

Bagwell, Philip S. (1982), *The Railwaymen*, Allen & Unwin.

Bagwell, Philip S. (1984), *The End of the Line*, Verso.

Barker, T. C. and Robbins, M. (1974), *A History of London Transport*, Vols 1 and 2, Allen & Unwin.

Blunkett, D. (1982), 'The Road to Cheap Fares', *Local Government Chronicle*, 23 April.

Bonavia, M. R. (1971), *The Organisation of British Railways*, Ian Allen.

British Railways Board (1963), *The Reshaping of British Railways* (The Beeching Report), HMSO.

Buchanan, Colin (1958), *Mixed Blessing: A Study of the Motor in Britain*, Leonard Hill.

Buchanan, Colin (Chairman) (1963), *Traffic in Towns*, HMSO.

Castells, Manuel (1978), *City Class and Power*, Macmillan.

Chester, N. (1975), *The Nationalisation of British Industry, 1945–51*, HMSO.

Davis, Emil (1908), *The Nationalisation of the Railways*

Department of the Environment (1973), *The Greater London Development Plan*, HMSO.

Department of Transport (1983), *Railway Finances* (The Serpell Report), HMSO.

Department of Transport (1984), White Paper *Buses*, Cmnd 9300, HMSO.

Department of Transport (Annual), *Transport Statistics Great Britain*, HMSO.

Gourvish, T. R. (1972), *Mark Huish and the London and North Western Railway*, Leicester University Press.

Greater Manchester Council (1983), *A Rail Strategy for Greater Manchester: The Options*, First Report of the Rail Study Group, Manchester City Council.

Greater Manchester Council (1983), *A Rail Strategy for Greater Manchester*, Second Report of the Rail Study Group, Manchester City Council.

Hamer, M. (1974), *Wheels within Wheels: A Study of the Road Lobby*, Friends of the Earth.

Hamer, M. (1984), 'Railroading London Motorways', *New Statesman*, 6 January.

Hillman, Mayer, with Irwin Henderson and Anne Whalley (1973), *Personal Mobility and Transport Policy*, Political and Economic Planning, Broadsheet No 542.

Hillman, Mayer, Irwin Henderson and Anne Whalley (1976), *Transport Realities and Planning Policies*, Political and Economic Planning.

Hillman, Mayer and Anne Whalley (1979), *Walking is Transport*, Policy Studies Institute.

Hillman, Mayer and Anne Whalley (1980), *The Social Consequences of Rail Closure*, Policy Studies Institute.

Hillman, Mayer and Anne Whalley (1983), *Energy and Personal Travel: Obstacles to Conservation*, Policy Studies Institute.

Howard, Ebenezer (1898), *To-morrow: A Peaceful Path to Real Reform*; revised edition (1902) retitled *Garden Cities of To-morrow*; current edition (1985) published by Attic Books, Eastbourne.

Hutchinson, G. E. (1983), 'The Role Metros can Play in Local Transport Networks (The Tyne and Wear Metro)', *Transport*, vol. 4, no. 1, pp. 10–11.

Jamieson, G. B., W. K. Mackay and J. C. R. Latchford (1967), 'Transportation and Land Use Structures', *Urban Studies*, vol. 4, no. 3, November.

Johnson, J. and Long, R. A. (1981), *British Railways Engineering, 1948–80* Mechanical Engineering Publications.

Kellett, J. R. (1969), The Impact of Railways on Victorian Cities, Routledge & Kegan Paul.

Klapper, Charles F. (1961), *The Golden Age of Tramways*, Routledge & Kegan Paul.

Lester, Nick and Stephen Potter (1983), *Vital Travel Statistics*, Transport 2000/ The Open University.

Ling, Arthur (1967), *Runcorn New Town*, Runcorn Development Corporation.

Llewelyn-Davies *et al.* (1970), *The Plan for Milton Keynes*, Milton Keynes Development Corporation.

Llewelyn-Davies *et al.* (1970), *The Plan for Milton Keynes, Transportation Technical Supplement*, Milton Keynes Development Corporation.

Markham, Sir Frank (1975), *A History of Milton Keynes and District, vol. 2 1800–1950*, White Crescent Press.

McKenna, F. (1980), *The Railway Workers, 1840–1970*, Faber & Faber.

Ministry of Transport (1947), *Government Control of Railways: Financial Returns 1940–46*, HMSO.

Morrison, Herbert (1933), *Socialisation and Transport*, Constable.

Morrison, Herbert (1938), *British Transport at Britain's Service*

Moseley, Malcolm (1979), *Accessibility: The Rural Challenge*, Methuen.

Painter, Martin (1980), 'Whitehall and Roads: A Case Study of Sectoral Politics', *Policy and Politics*, vol. 8, no. 2.

Perkins, H. (1970), *The Age of the Railways*, Panther.

Plowden, William (1971), *The Motor Car and Politics, 1896–1970*, Bodley Head.

Potter, Stephen (1981), *Transport Planning in the Garden Cities*, The Open University, New Towns Study Unit.

Potter, Stephen (1982), 'The Transport Policy Crisis', Unit 27 of Open University Course *D202 Urban Change and Conflict*, The Open University Press.

Potter, Stephen (1983), 'Energy Conservation in Transport in Rural and Island Communities', pp. 423–30 of Twidell, J. *et al.*, *Energy for Rural and Island Communities III*, Pergamon.

Potter, Stephen and Ray Thomas (1982), 'The New Town Experience', Unit 28a of Open University Course *D202 Urban Change and Conflict*, The Open University Press.

Serpell Report (1983), see Department of Transport.

Simmons, J. (1961), *The Railways of Britain*, Routledge & Kegan Paul.

Starkie, D. (1982), *The Motorway Age*, Pergamon Press.

Steadman, Julian (1983), 'Urban Form and Public Transport', unpublished MA Thesis, University of Nottingham.

Transport and Environment Studies (TEST) (1983), *Investing in British Rail*, TEST report for Transport 2000.

Transport and Environment Studies (TEST) (1984), *BR: A European Railway*, TEST report No. 51 for Transport 2000.

Transport and Environment Studies (TEST) (1985), *The Company Car Factor*, TEST report for the London Amenity and Transport Association.

Wilson, H. and L. Womersley (1966), *Redditch New Town*, Redditch Development Corporation.

Wistrich, Enid (1983), *The Politics of Transport*, Longman.

Woollett, Stephen (1981), *Alternative Rural Services*, National Council of Voluntary Organisations.

Index